Design and Construction

During the 1930s, Britain had begun to re-arm, but at the start of the Second World War the Royal Navy was still desperately short of ships of all sizes, in particular destroyers. Only a limited number of shipyards had the facilities and capabilities to build fleet destroyers (see ShipCraft 21), and they were expensive and took a long time to design and build. Nor were they ideally suited to all the tasks they were asked to perform, particularly escorting slow merchant ships. There was an explosion in the construction of corvettes (see ShipCraft Flower class Special) and sloops and frigates (see ShipCraft 26) to carry out this task, but the vessels were generally slow. The Admiralty identified a need for faster craft, with good anti-aircraft and anti-submarine armament, and so, in 1938, was born the idea of a vessel with sufficient speed for fleet duties (at least 25 knots, hence requiring steam turbine machinery) combined with the armament of the *Black Swan* class sloops, which eventually became the 'Hunt' class escort destroyer. The bottlenecks in the production of gun mountings resulted in the selection of the Mk XVI 4in HA/LA gun on the Mk XIX twin mounting for the main armament.

At the end of the First world War, there was a surplus of destroyers, and between the wars many were scrapped. Those that did survive were modified to help to fill the escort gap and fifty WWI-era destroyers were obtained from America, which became the 'Town' class. Also, some of the destroyers built since WWI, the 'A' to 'I' classes (see ShipCraft 11), were also employed, some remaining as built (but usually with additional AA armament) and others modified to make them more suitable for escorting convoys.

'HUNT' CLASS

In 1938, the Chief of the Naval Staff directed that consideration should be given to a new design of 'Fast Escort Vessel',

Left: The twin 4in mounting was a highly valued medium calibre AA gun. Not only did it form the primary armament of the 'Hunt' class destroyers, the 'WAIR' conversions and the *Black Swan* class sloops, but was also the main heavy AA weapon in many cruisers and capital ships. This is a gunshop photo of the Mk XIX mounting.

mounting 4in guns but no torpedoes. Preliminary discussions preferred six 4in guns but, in the interests of economy, deemed that four would be acceptable, and so sketch designs were prepared by two different constructors. Both designs were to carry four 4in guns and also four torpedo tubes, one, at 265ft lwl, being 25ft longer than the other. In September, these designs were discussed, and it was decided there should be six 4in guns and no torpedo tubes, but the vessels should include depth charges, Asdic and stabilisers.

In October, the First Sea Lord stated that they should have an endurance of 2500 miles at 20 knots and that officers' accommodation was to be forward for easy access to the bridge. In November, a Legend of Particulars for a vessel of 278ft overall length was presented to the Admiralty Board, and on 1 December it was approved. Later that month, it was noted that first priority for the 4in gun mountings would be for five AA conversions of the WWI 'V&W' class destroyers, the second priority being the first 20 'Fast Escort Vessels'.

Approval was given for the construction of just ten vessels whilst consideration was given to an alternative design with four 4in guns and a triple or quadruple torpedo tube mounting. Tenders were requested on 20 December, for a response just one

Above: Three profiles, clearly showing the differences in armament between the first three types of 'Hunt' class destroyers: Type 1 *Berkeley*, with two twin 4in mountings; Type 2 *Bramham*, with three twin 4in mountings; Type 3 *Goathland*, with two twin 4in mountings and twin torpedo tubes.

Right: The launch of *Atherstone* at Cammell Laird's shipyard on 12 December 1939, six months after being laid down and 15 months before completion, the extended period being due to the changes necessary because of the error made when calculating her stability.

month later. The shipbuilders did raise some questions regarding the estimated weights and, after a question from Yarrow's regarding stability, it was decided to increase the beam by 6in. The Director of Naval Construction (DNC) subsequently increased the beam by another 3in to 29ft. The first ten were ordered on 21 March 1939 and the First Sea Lord directed that the second batch of ten would be to the same design, these being ordered on 11 April. The successful tenders varied between £284,000 and £287,000, excluding armament.

In February 1940, the First Lord, Winston Churchill, issued the directive that the new vessels should be termed destroyers, even though the first two groups did not carry torpedo tubes, one of the normal characteristics of a destroyer.

When the first vessel, *Atherstone*, was nearing completion, an inclining experiment was carried out and it was discovered that the GM was 1 foot less than calculated, a serious error. As a result, No 2 twin 4in mounting had to be landed, top weight reduced and 52 tons of ballast added. By this time, the third batch of vessels had been ordered and the first three were too far advanced for any major modifications, and so received the same changes.

The twenty-three Type 1 destroyers therefore generally commissioned with two twin 4in gun mountings, a quadruple 2pdr pom-pom on the aft superstructure, two Lewis guns in the bridge wings, two depth charge throwers and one rail (40 depth charges). Radar was not available when the destroyers completed but was added during subsequent refits, although the majority did carry Type 285 on the fire control director at an early stage. Some of the Type 1s, for example *Blencathra*, completed with a Holman Projector on a platform over the boiler room vents, whilst others, like *Whaddon*, received an athwartships platform for two single 20mm Oerlikon guns in that position. The guns were not available when *Whaddon* completed and may have been replaced with shielded Lewis guns, as in *Liddesdale*.

The thirty-six Type 2 destroyers had their beam increased by 2½ft to 31½ft, permitting the originally intended installation of six 4in guns. Both the bridge and the funnel were also lowered, and the ballast was removed. AA armament was increased by the inclusion of two single 20mm Oerlikon guns in the bridge wings. A/S armament was also increased with the addition of a second depth charge rail (110 depth charges).

Below: This starboard quarter view of *Farndale*, launched by Swan Hunter in September 1940, clearly shows the two after twin 4in mountings and the transom stern. Note, it was usual to carry pennant numbers on the transom.

The first twenty destroyers of this type were ordered in September 1939 and the remainder followed in December. Radar was fitted when available, but many had to wait until they received a refit.

Meetings in March and May 1940 decided that the Type 3 destroyers would suppress the aft 4in mounting and be fitted with a twin 21in torpedo tube, retaining the same dimensions and machinery as the Type 2s. A third single 20mm Oerlikon gun was fitted on the quarterdeck and the number of depth charge throwers increased to four. In order to achieve this, 40 tons of ballast were installed. The funnel was altered, being vertical with a cowl, in order to make it more difficult for the enemy to estimate the inclination of the destroyer.

Twelve were ordered in July 1940 and sixteen the following month. When completed, these destroyers carried Type 291 warning radar, Type 285 fire control radar and Type 128 sonar.

In 1938 Sir John I Thornycroft presented a proposal for a '1000 ton destroyer'. The designs were criticised by the DNC and no further action was taken. The proposal was revived in March 1940 following a visit by Admiral Fraser, Third Sea Lord and Controller, to Thornycroft's shipyard. Following further submissions, and criticisms, a design with a continuous shelter deck, partially enclosed bridge, six 4in guns and a quadruple torpedo tube was accepted, and the two Type 4 destroyers were ordered in July 1940, at the same time as four Type 3 destroyers. In August, DNC specified that the quadruple torpedo tubes were to be replaced by a triple mounting with power training.

Their waterline length was 11ft greater than the Type 2 vessels and the waterline breadth 1ft 10in greater. The flare at the bow was continued aft and a short chine added, increasing dryness. Displacement increased and 55 tons of ballast were carried. The cost of the hulls increased by approximately £12,000. Endurance was 2350 nm at 20 knots. Both the smaller calibre AA and the A/S armament remained the same, although the number of depth charges carried was reduced to just 50.

All four types were propelled by a twin shaft arrangement, driven by Parsons impulse reaction, single reduction turbines, powered by two Admiralty 3-drum boilers. The turbines produced 19,000shp at 380rpm and the boilers operated at a pressure of 300 lbs/sq in. This resulted in the Type 1 destroyers having a nominal top speed of 28 knots, the wider Type 2 and Type 3 destroyers a nominal top speed of 27 knots and the heavier Type 4 destroyers a nominal top speed of 25 knots. Torsion meters were only fitted to a few vessels of each type during trials, and gave readings slightly in excess of the nominal 19,000 horsepower. Speeds were measured in a number of different ways, not on a measured mile, with the first ship, *Atherstone*, being credited with 30.25 knots, although the majority of trial speeds were slightly below the nominal speed. The earlier vessels were fitted with stabilisers but these were not a great success, and many of the later ones received additional stowage for fuel oil instead.

One change common to many – eighteen Type 1 (including *Atherstone*, *Berkeley*, *Cleveland*, *Cotswold*, *Fernie*, *Hambledon*, *Holderness*, *Liddesdale*, *Meynell*, *Southdown* and *Whaddon*), seven Type 2 (*Avon Vale*, *Bedale*, *Calpe*, *Cowdray*, *Krakowiak* (ex-*Silverton*), *Lamerton* and *Lauderdale*), and six Type 3 (*Albrighton*, *Bleasdale*, *Eskdale*, *Glaisdale*, *Stevenstone* and *La Combattante*) – was the addition of a single 2pdr gun right forward, usually known as a 'bow chaser', which was used particularly for engaging *schnellboote* and other small craft at close quarters. Destroyers converted as small headquarters ships for the Normandy landings also received the same mounting.

Below: *Liddersdale*, launched by Vickers-Armstrong in August 1940, shows the 2pdr 'bow chaser' gun for engaging *schnellboote* and other small craft, right forward.

Above: This aerial view of *Derwent*, launched by Vickers-Armstrong in August 1941, shows the torpedo tubes mounted amidships and the very congested quarterdeck, fitted with depth charge throwers and rails, and smoke floats fitted on top of the rails.

'TOWN' CLASS

The possibility of obtaining destroyers from America was first raised in May 1940. In August, President Roosevelt proposed the transfer of fifty old destroyers in return for the sale of base rights. Churchill rejected this proposal but proposed the lease of base rights, and on 1 September the transfer was agreed. Two of the ships to be transferred had been deleted from the US Navy List and the others were either in reserve or active service.

Three of the destroyers were of the *Caldwell* class, twenty-seven of the *Wickes* class and twenty of the *Clemson* class. All were to be commissioned by the USN and sailed to Halifax, Nova Scotia, where after just three days' familiarisation, they would be commissioned into the Royal Navy, retaining their American names. However, in September, it was decided to rename them after towns common to Great Britain and America.

The three classes were very similar in size (lwl 310ft), although the top speed of the *Caldwell* class, at 30 knots, was 5 knots less than the others. The *Caldwell* class were originally designed with three shafts with direct drive turbines, and three funnels, but only three were completed to that design, two of which were transferred to Great Britain, as *Leeds* (ex-*Conner*) and *Ludlow* (ex-*Stockton*). The remainder of the class, and the other two classes, had twin shafts with geared turbines, and four funnels. Main armament was four 4in/50cal guns and twelve 21in torpedo tubes. Secondary armament of the early boats was two 1pdr guns but these were replaced by 3in/23cal guns in the later ships.

A report compiled while the first ships were in Halifax noted a number of problems and made recommendations, but when the destroyers arrived in Great Britain there was limited time available for modifications and so they were often incorporated gradually, rather than all at the same time. The first alterations were the removal of the mainmast and shortening the foremast, reducing the height of the three after funnels, and the removal of the two after sets of torpedo tubes. These significantly

Above: *Brecon*, the first of two Type 4 'Hunt' class destroyers to be launched, showing the extended forecastle and the forward chine, both of which improved seakeeping.

Below: This photograph of the Type 2 destroyer *Lauderdale* in 1942 clearly shows her camouflage pattern and the 2pdr 'bow chaser' mounting. Note the fire control director is positioned with the Type 285 radar pointing aft, action commonly taken to protect the antenna from damage by spray.

reduced top weight and improved stability; 50 tons of ballast was added also. The aft 4in and 3in guns were removed and replaced with a 12pdr HA mounting; depth charge throwers were added, as was Asdic, if not already fitted.

The depth charge rails were re-oriented fore and aft, requiring sponsons, and some changes were also made to the ships' boats, landing some and replacing them with Royal Navy types. Royal Navy type davits also replaced the American ones. The propeller guards were strengthened and, in some cases, moved.

Bradford (ex-*McLanahan*), *Clare* (ex-*Abel P Upshur*) and *Stanley* (ex-*McCalla*), because of their poor condition, were immediately converted into long range escorts, which involved the removal of the two forward boilers and funnels, and their replacement with additional bunkerage. New superstructures, including the bridge, were constructed and the beam 4in guns replaced by single 2pdr mountings. Two 20mm Oerlikon guns were installed and a triple torpedo tube. The number of depth charge throwers was increased to eight, with two depth charge rails; the first two also receiving a Hedgehog mortar, but not until a year after the initial conversions. Type 271 surface-search radar was fitted on the bridge, but no air-warning radar.

Not all vessels received identical modifications. Below are just a few examples:

Bath (ex-*Hopewell*) did not have her funnels cut-down and retained her aft 4in and 3in guns, but did have her aft torpedo tubes removed.

Belmont (ex-*Satterlee*) and *Broadwater* (ex-*Mason*) received a Type 286 air-search radar at the masthead.

Brighton (ex-*Cowell*) received a Type 271 radar on her bridge and Type 291 search radar at her masthead. Her wing 4in guns were replaced with 20mm mountings and her beam torpedo tubes replaced with a triple centreline mounting.

Burwell (ex-*Laub*) retained her beam 4in guns and torpedo tubes, but did receive a Type 286 radar, and 20mm guns sited between the first and second funnels.

Caldwell (ex-*Hale*) did not have her funnels cut down but did have her mainmast and aft torpedo tubes removed, whilst retaining her aft 4in gun.

Campbeltown (ex-*Buchanan*) had the mainmast removed, but only the aft funnel

Below: *Crowninshield* (renamed *Chelsea* in RN service) was a member of the *Wickes* class, and here is shown while still in US Navy service. Note the mainmast aft.

Above: *Newport* (ex-*Sigourney* of the *Wickes* class), in 1941, has had her aft three funnels reduced in height; she carries the fixed antenna of a Type 286 radar at her masthead, but retains her beam 4in guns. The ship was transferred to the Royal Norwegian Navy in March 1941 and is seen here flying the Norwegian ensign.

was reduced in height. The aft 4in and 3in mountings were removed and replaced by a 12pdr HA mounting on the aft superstructure. The aft torpedo tubes were removed and replaced by two depth charge throwers. The depth charge racks were aligned fore and aft and the propeller guards replaced by some at deck level; 0.5in machine guns were mounted forward of the two midships 4in mountings, and the bridge roof searchlight removed.

Castleton (ex-*Aaron Ward*) received the minimum of modifications – the mainmast was removed but the funnels were not cut-down; the after torpedo tubes were removed; one boat was landed and carley

Right: *Lincoln,* (ex-*Yarnell* of the *Wickes* class), has her Hedgehog mortar, aft of 'A' mounting, protected by a tarpaulin. Note the propeller guards at the stern have been raised.

floats added; the two 4in guns were retained, as was the 3in, but no additional AA armament was added.

Leeds (ex-*Conner*) was one of the destroyers with just three funnels and had her forward mounting replaced by two single 2pdr mountings whilst retaining her 4in/50 guns astern and on the beam. No torpedo tubes were carried but 20mm guns were fitted in a bandstand aft, and a Type 286 radar at her masthead.

Ludlow (ex-*Stockton*) carried two single 2pdr mountings forward in lieu of the 3in gun, but retained her beam and aft guns. 20mm mountings were fitted on a bandstand at the stern. The funnels of both *Leeds* and *Ludlow* had half-height casings.

Mansfield (ex-*Evans*) had her aft torpedo tubes and guns removed, together with her mainmast. A 12pdr mounting was fitted aft and 0.5in machine guns abeam the funnels.

Newport (ex-*Sigourney*) was similarly modified, but all torpedo tubes were removed and replaced by a centreline triple mounting, and the three aft funnels reduced in height. A 20mm Oerlikon was mounted on a platform immediately aft of the searchlight tower and Type 286 radar mounted at the mast head.

Niagara (ex-*Thatcher*) had her beam torpedo tubes removed and a 12pdr mounting added aft, but few other changes.

Reading (ex-*Bailey*) had her bridge cut down and 0.5in machine guns fitted on top, the after torpedo tubes and mainmast removed, and a 12pdr gun fitted aft. The funnels were not shortened.

Ripley (ex-*Shubrick*) had a Type 286 radar, but her funnels were not reduced in height initially. Later, they were shortened and a cowl added to the forefunnel.

St Clair (ex-*Williams*) did not have her funnels shortened but did have her mainmast and aft torpedo tubes removed. She retained her aft 4in gun.

St Francis (ex-*Bancroft*) had her mainmast reduced to a stump and her aft three funnels shortened. She received Type 286 radar and a 12pdr gun aft, but lost her torpedo tubes.

'V&W' CLASS

A total of 70 'V' and 'W' class destroyers were built, either during the First World War or in the years immediately after. This included five that were classed as 'Leaders', twenty-five 'V' class vessels, twenty-one 'W' class vessels and nineteen Modified 'W' class vessels. Many more were cancelled when the war ended.

Below: *Ripley* (ex-*Shubrick* of the *Clemson* class) has an HF/DF mast aft as well as radar Type 271 on the bridge. Her funnels have been shortened and a cowl added to the forefunnel.

Above: *Stanley* (ex-*McCalla* of the *Clemson* class) displays her rebuilt bridge with the lantern of radar Type 271 on the top. As converted to an LRE, she retained only the two after funnels.

The dimensions of all these destroyers were the same – loa 312ft with 29ft 6in beam (except the 'Specials' that were slightly wider at 30ft 8½in) – and they came to be listed as one 'V&W' class. A twin shaft propulsion system driven by geared turbines resulted in a top speed of 34 knots.

Main armament was four 4in/45cal Mk V guns for the earlier destroyers, but the calibre was increased to 4.7in for the Modified 'W' class. The 'Leaders' and the 'V' class were fitted with two twin 21in torpedo tubes, and the later ones with triple tubes. AA armament also increased from two single 40mm (2pdr) pom-poms in the 'Leaders' to a single 3in gun in the later vessels.

With the advent of WWII, a number of different modifications were carried out to suit these destroyers for their new roles. However, ten destroyers – four of them in Australian service – were little altered. Commonly, 'Y' mounting was removed and replaced with depth charges, but few other changes. Five of these vessels were lost in 1940, one in 1941, and three in 1942.

The modifications were given three designations – WAIR (possibly from 'W' class anti-AIRcraft), LRE (long range escorts) and SRE (short range escorts). The vessels modified under each classification were similar but not identical.

Fifteen destroyers and one leader received WAIR modifications. The machinery was unaltered, but the armament was changed to two twin 4in Mk XVI mountings and two quadruple 0.5in machine gun mountings. Type 285 radar was usually carried on the gun director, but *Vanity* had it missing in 1940. By 1942 two 20mm Oerlikons had been added in the bridge wings, and the 0.5in mountings had been replaced by 20mm mountings in most of the destroyers. The leader, *Wallace*, being larger, also received a quadruple 2pdr pom-pom when first converted, and two additional single 2pdr mountings by 1944.

Nineteen destroyers were modified as SREs, including *Broke* and *Keppel*, both of the 'Shakespeare' class, and *Campbell*, *Douglas*, *Mackay* and *Montrose* of the 'Scott' class, but their armament differed significantly. The main changes were to increase their AA armament, whilst retaining some of the original 4.7in mountings. In some,

Above: *Vampire* is shown in January 1932, having undergone only a few modifications since being launched in 1917. She was transferred to Australia in 1933, and sunk by Japanese aircraft whilst escorting the aircraft carrier *Hermes* in April 1942.

Below: *Vanity* after undergoing her WAIR conversion. As well as the twin 4in guns, the quadruple 0.5in mountings can be seen between the aft funnel and the searchlight platform.

but not all, cases, the torpedo tubes were removed.

Whitshed, *Witherington* and *Wivern* each retained two 4.7in guns and both sets of torpedo tubes (not *Witherington*) and received two single 2pdr guns, and between two and six 20mm guns.

Malcolm, *Veteran* and *Wolverine* retained two 4.7in guns and one set of torpedo tubes. They had a 12pdr AA gun in lieu of the torpedo tubes and a Hedgehog mortar in lieu of 'A' mounting. 'Y' mounting was replaced by depth charges. They were also fitted with Type 271 radar. *Veteran* also carried Type 276 radar at her masthead, but this was soon replaced.

Windsor and *Walpole* received a twin 6pdr (in lieu of 'A' gun) and three 2pdr mountings plus two 20mm guns.

Wishart and *Witch* retained three and two, respectively, 4.7in guns, with a 12pdr AA gun but no torpedo tubes.

Below: *Vanessa*, after conversion to an LRE, carries a Type 271 radar lantern on the bridge roof, and is painted in an Admiralty camouflage scheme.

Worcester retained four 4.7in guns and one set of torpedo tubes. She also carried a 12pdr and two 2pdr AA mountings and two 20mm guns.

Vivacious was the same as *Worcester* but with three 4in guns in lieu of the 4.7in guns.

By 1942, the majority of unaltered destroyers were spending most of their time on convoy escort duties and were considered as SREs. Although they did not receive a full refit, some minor changes were made to them. See MODIFICATIONS section later.

The conversion to LRE, of which there were twenty, required more radical changes, the primary one being the removal of the forward funnel and boiler, with the boiler room being converted into a fuel tank. In the majority, the forward gun mounting was replaced by a Hedgehog ASW mortar, and a number of single 20mm Oerlikon mountings were added. Type 271 radar was fitted on the bridge roof, with Type 291 at the masthead. As with the SREs, there were many variations in the armament outfit. The typical fit was two or three 4in or 4.7in guns, two or three 2pdr AA mountings and four or five 20mm guns. Some, including *Viscount*, *Vimy* and *Watchman*, had the torpedo tube mounting replaced by a 12pdr AA gun.

Other Royal Navy destroyers that survived from the First World War are listed below.

'R' CLASS

Skate, built by John Brown, was the only surviving vessel of this class of thirty-nine. There had also been some Thornycroft and Yarrow 'Specials' but none had survived, nor had any of the eleven 'Modified R' class. At 276ft overall length, these destroyers carried three 4in and one 2pdr guns, and two twin torpedo tubes. A twin screw, geared drive gave them a speed of 36 knots. *Skate* had her midships 4in gun replaced by two 20mm guns, and a 12pdr AA gun replaced the 2pdr and the torpedo tubes. Type 286 radar was fitted at her masthead, and she carried four depth charge throwers and two rails on the quarterdeck.

'S' CLASS

A total of 67 'S' class destroyers were built, the majority being launched in 1918 (although the first was actually launched in 1916); eleven more were launched in 1919 and just one in 1920. They were originally armed with three 4in guns, a 2pdr pom-pom and two twin 21in torpedo tubes. There were three different variants – the basic Admiralty design, seven 'Specials'

Opposite: *Wolverine* in 1942 shows her layout as an SRE, retaining 'B' and 'X' gun mountings and the forward triple torpedo tubes. The aft tubes have been replaced by a 12pdr AA mounting, and Hedgehog is fitted forward. The two 20mm Oerlikon guns can be seen on a platform between the funnels.

Below: This port quarter view of *Skate* in December 1942 shows the 12pdr AA gun aft of the funnels and two 20mm guns on a platform aft.

Above: A starboard quarter view of *Scimitar* in 1940 shows the very heavy load of depth charges carried after her conversion for escort duties.

from Yarrow and three 'Specials' from Thornycroft. None of the 'Specials' survived to serve in WWII but eleven of the Admiralty design did – *Scimitar* and *Scout* built by John Brown; *Sabre, Saladin* and *Sardonyx* built by Alexander Stephen; *Shikari* built by Doxford; *Stronghold* and *Sturdy* built by Scott; *Tenedos, Thanet* and *Thracian* built by Hawthorn Leslie.

Five of them were sent to Singapore and another, *Sturdy*, was held in the Mediterranean on her way to the Far East. These vessels received few modifications. Those that remained in Home Waters (*Sardonyx, Sabre, Scimitar, Saladin, Shikari* and *Skate*) were converted to ASW escorts in late 1940. Two of the 4in guns were removed, as were the two twin torpedo tubes. Two depth charge rails and eight throwers were added, together with one 12pdr AA gun and two quadruple 0.5in mountings. The complement increased by nearly 50 per cent, the total weight of all these additions being much greater than that of the equipment removed.

They were all of a twin shaft design, 276ft long, and initially capable of 36 knots.

'SCOTT' CLASS FLOTILLA LEADERS

Eight of these vessels were built and six served in the Second World War – *Douglas, Campbell, Malcolm* and *Mackay* built by Cammell Laird; and *Stuart* and *Montrose* built by Hawthorn Leslie, the former having been taken over by Australia in 1933.

They were also a twin shaft design initially capable of 36 knots, but were larger at 332ft 6in oa. Their armament was also greater with five 4.7in, a 3in AA and two 2pdr pom-pom guns and six 21in torpedo tubes.

These ships received few modifications between the wars. Early in WWII *Douglas* had the amidships 4.7in gun replaced by two 2pdr pom-pom mountings, with the aft funnel being shortened to improve the field of fire for the 3in anti-aircraft gun. Later, three Oerlikon 20mm guns were fitted, and a further two Oerlikons finally replaced the 2pdrs. Radar (Type 286, later replaced by Type 290, and Type 271) was fitted during the war, as was HF/DF radio direction-finding gear.

Campbell, Mackay and *Montrose* received the same initial modifications, and in 1941/42, 'X' mounting was removed and replaced by the 3in anti-aircraft gun, taken from its original amidships position. Both sets of torpedo tubes were retained. Two Oerlikon 20mm guns were mounted on the bridge wings, while further Oerlikon guns later replaced the 2pdr pom-poms. They received the same radar outfit.

For *Campbell*, conversion to a short-range escort involved removal of two more 4.7in guns and a bank of torpedo tubes, with the forward gun replaced by a Hedgehog anti-submarine mortar, and the aft gun and tubes removed to allow a heavy depth charge armament of 70 charges. *Mackay* and *Montrose* retained both sets of torpedo tubes, and were fitted to launch a 10-depth charge pattern. Type 271 radar was mounted above the bridge, replacing the low-angle director and associated rangefinder, while Type 291 radar was mounted at the top of the mast. In 1943, a twin 6pdr replaced the forward 4.7in gun, for use against German S-boats.

When *Stuart* entered RAN service in 1933, her armament consisted of five 4.7in guns, a QF 3in anti-aircraft gun, two 2pdr pom-poms, six 21in torpedo tubes (in two triple mountings), two depth charge chutes, and four depth charge throwers. By 1941, two of the 4.7in guns had been removed, five 20mm Oerlikon guns and a Breda gun had been fitted, and the depth charge chutes were replaced with depth charge rails. A year later, a third 4.7in gun was removed, along with two of the Oerlikons, the Breda gun, and the torpedo tubes. During 1942, a Hedgehog anti-submarine mortar was installed. When she was later converted into a stores ship and troop transport in 1944, her armament was changed to a single 4in gun, seven Oerlikons, three quad-barrelled pom-poms, and a Hedgehog.

'SHAKESPEARE' CLASS FLOTILLA LEADERS

Five of this class were built to a Thornycroft design, being 329ft long, with similar machinery and mounting the same armament as the 'Scott' class. *Wallace*, *Keppel* and *Broke* (launched as *Rooke*) served in the Second World War.

Wallace underwent a WAIR conversion at Devonport Dockyard between September 1938 and June 1939, similar to that of the 'V&W' class but her larger size allowed a quadruple 2pdr pom-pom mount to be fitted right aft. Anti-aircraft armament was completed by two quadruple Vickers 0.5in mounts amidships where the torpedo tubes were previously mounted, with the forward mount on the port side and the aft mount to starboard. Modern sonar, and a relatively powerful depth-charge outfit of 30 depth charges provided the ship's anti-submarine equipment. No torpedo tubes were fitted.

Broke and *Keppel* retained two 4.7in guns ('B' and 'X' mountings), and two triple

Below: A starboard quarter view of *Douglas*, in September 1943, shows the direction-finding antenna on a pole mast aft, and the depth charge rails. Note the smoke floats lashed to the top of the rails.

Above: *Stuart* in September 1943 shows well-worn paintwork. She carries a Hedgehog mortar forward and Type 271 radar on her bridge, whilst retaining two 4.7in gun mountings. Amidships is a 12pdr AA gun.

torpedo tubes, and gained a 3in and four 20mm AA guns. They also received a Hedgehog mortar and depth charges. Both ships received Type 273 radar for gun fire control and Type 291 radar at the mast-head.

NETHERLANDS Z5 CLASS

The four torpedo boats of the *Z5* class were launched in 1915. Following the German invasion, they all reached England in May 1940. They were 191ft 10in long, had a maximum speed of 27 knots when first built, and were armed with two 75mm guns and four 450mm torpedo tubes. *Z5* was converted to a patrol vessel in 1930, when her torpedo tubes, a boiler and her forward funnel were removed, and her forecastle lengthened. Her maximum speed was reduced to 22 knots and, in March 1942, she was taken over by the Royal Navy as *Blade*, eventually being sold in 1945 and broken-up at Troon.

Right: This photograph of *Wallace* clearly shows the protection around the forward twin 4in gun mounting. This was required because of the low freeboard forward, which frequently led to the destroyer shipping 'green seas'.

Model Products

NAVIS NEPTUN

1:1250 scale

This German company (Navis Modellbau) was founded in 1962, their range now including more than 1000 models. It is not possible to keep all models in production simultaneously, so it is sometimes necessary to wait for a specific model to become available. All models are waterline, cast in metal and hand finished. They are painted grey overall, with a few highlights, such as funnel tops painted black.

The range currently includes: 1167, a Type 2 'Hunt' class; 1167a, a Type 1 'Hunt' class; 1167c, a Type 4 'Hunt' class; 1169, a WAIR type conversion; 1169a HMS *Vivien*; 1169b, HMS *Vansittart*; 1169c, HMS *Wivern*; 161aN, HMS *Vanoc*; 162N, 'S' class; and 163bN, 'R' class.

SEAVEE

1:1250 scale

SeaVee Models, from France, is operated by Sean Pritchard. The masters are prepared by hand and a limited number of metal castings taken. These are finished by hand, using etched brass where appropriate (*eg* for lattice masts and bridge wing supports) and hand painted. This approach and the detailed research does provide the opportunity for the same basic casting to be completed in slightly varying configurations with different camouflage schemes.

The range has included a number of Royal Navy destroyers surviving from the First World War and the ex-US 'Town' class.

AJM MODELS

1:700 & 1:350 scale

This Polish company produces a number of different resin kits of the 'Scott' class Flotilla Leaders, both at 1:700 and 1:350 scale. The first kit at 1:350 scale represents the ships as built, the second HMAS *Stuart* as in 1941–1942, the third HMS *Douglas* as in 1942 and the fourth HMS *Malcolm*, also as in 1942. At 1:700 scale AJM produce the same models, plus HMS *Mackay* as in 1945 and HMS *Campbell* as in 1942. Apart from size, the main difference between the kits at the two scales is that the larger models are full hull, although split at the waterline, whilst the smaller ones are waterline only. The kits of both scales are supplied in robust card boxes.

For the 1:350 scale kits, some cleaning-up of the two hull parts is required before they can be joined. The 1:350 scale kits include three plastic bags of resin parts, a large sheet of etched brass containing railings, ladders, davits, funnel grilles, depth charge racks, open boat details and shields for the 20mm guns, plus two small sheets for the main calibre guns and a further sheet representing splinter mat protection to be placed around the bridge area. There are also lengths of different diameter brass rods for the masts, some very fine anchor chain and turned brass barrels for the main calibre guns. Finally, there is a small decal sheet with a white ensign, a union jack, white depth markings and gold name-boards, and pennant numbers where applicable. A very complete set of parts but the resin parts do have substantial 'pours' on them that will require careful removal.

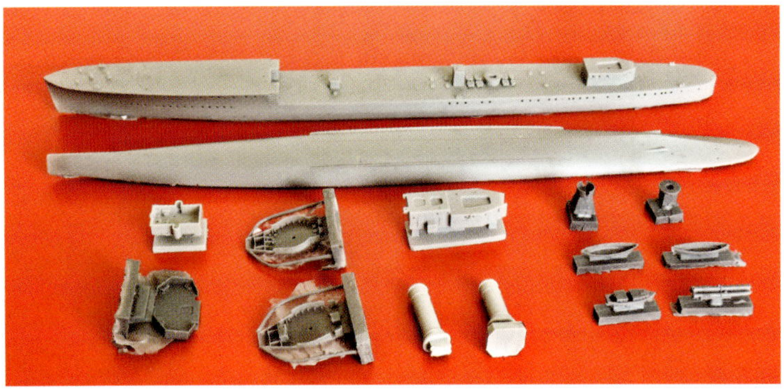

The instructions are not extensive but they are clear, although great attention is required not to miss any of the smaller parts. The etched brass items are identified by numbers etched into the sheet but no identifications of their purpose are given – this would be a nice touch, particularly when referring to the armament, as no technical details of the original vessel are given.

The instructions do include a colour scheme, the paints being identified from the LifeColor series. As these are standard Western Approaches colours, common to many other ships, alternatives can be easily found.

Similar comments apply to the 1:700 scale kits, but with the many small parts, the removal of the large 'pours' presents even more of a problem. There are no brass gun barrels or anchor chain.

AOSHIMA

1:700 scale

A plastic model of an 'S' class destroyer is provided by Aoshima as part of one of their 'County' class cruiser kits, HMS *Cornwall* (Item 056721). It comprises four light grey sprues, the smallest one, containing details such as depth charge throwers, being duplicated. The waterline hull is provided in two parts, with base plate and two-part deck. The mouldings are detailed and clean, with no flash, but the attachment points to the sprues are thick.

The colour scheme given is grey all over, with the deck being a different colour to the sides and superstructure. Paint colours are quoted from the Aqueous Hobby Color and Mr Color ranges, both from the GSI Creos Corporation.

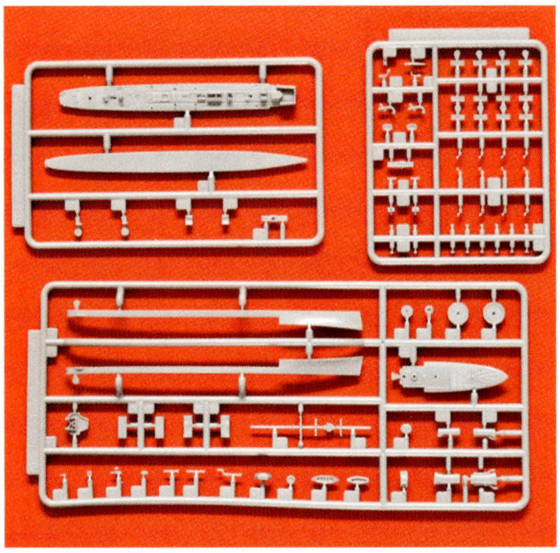

ARROWMODEL

1:700 scale

This model from America represents HMS *Vanity* after her WAIR conversion. It comprises a resin waterline hull moulding and superstructure parts, with white metal gun mountings, boats and davits.

Instructions are on a single double-sided sheet, with text on one side and illustrations on the other. The text begins with a small amount of history and technical information, and is followed by the assembly instructions. The main assembly drawing shows a number of alternatives, including alternative bridge wings to represent HMS *Winchester* and additional 20mm guns (not supplied) after 1942. It also points out that the large weather shield forward should be cut down to represent HMS *Vanity*. The kit appears to try and represent many different vessels and so research is required to accurately depict a particular vessel. The resin parts are well moulded and include four funnels, three short thick ones and one taller thin one. There is a very fine etched brass sheet which includes railings and davits. The white metal castings are very basic so, as well as the research mentioned above, after-market parts will be needed to produce a model to modern standards.

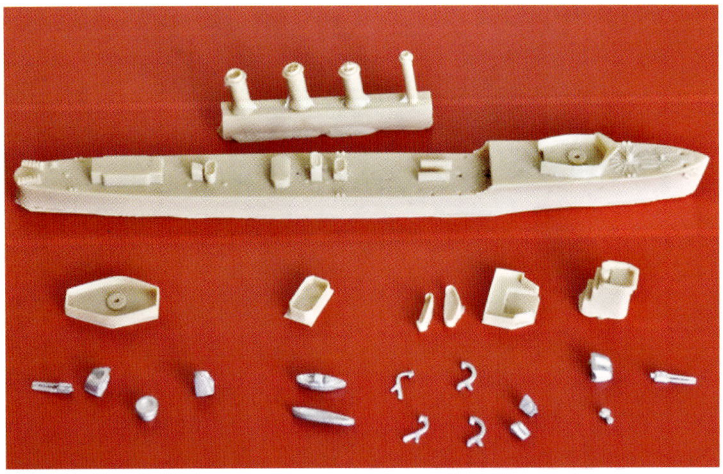

The instructions do include a reduced (black and white) reproduction of the colour image of *Vanity* in the book Man o'War 2 and some very small photographs (black and white) of *Vanity* in June 1942, with a different camouflage pattern.

B-RESINA

1:700 scale

B-Resina models have ceased production but the range included kits for the Type 1 'Hunt' class destroyer HMS *Fernie*, the Type 2 destroyer, HMS *Badsworth*, and the 'Town' class destroyers, HMS *Burwell* and HMS *Campbeltown*.

Earlier models contained a resin waterline hull and white metal details/accessories. Later models were cast entirely in resin. Instructions were simple, containing assembly drawings and details of the brass wire required for masts, and colour details. The model of HMS *Campbeltown* represents the destroyer as modified for the raid on St Nazaire. These were simple models but basically accurate. With the addition of etched brass and some replacement components, they can be brought up to the standards expected today.

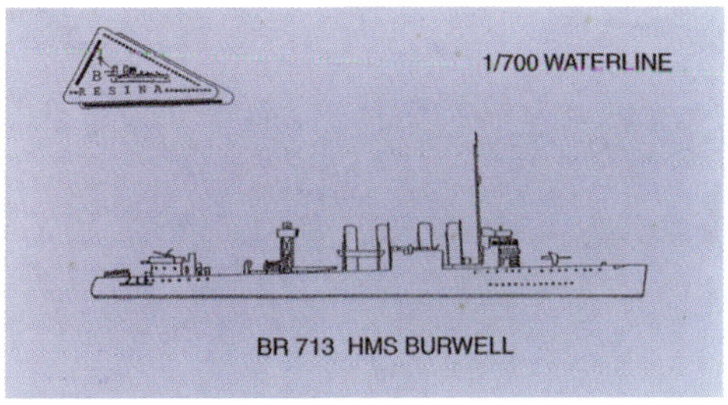

CHOROSZY MODELBUD

1:700 scale

This Polish company have produced a finely cast, resin model of ORP *Krakowiak* (ex-HMS *Silverton*) moulded in an unusual, dark green colour. In addition to the waterline hull there are two bags of resin mouldings, one containing the larger superstructure parts and the other containing the smaller details. There is an etched brass sheet and turned brass gun barrels.

Instructions are supplied on one A4 sheet and one A3 sheet. The A4 sheet contains an enlarged image of the etched brass sheet and technical details (in Polish) on one side, and historical details and basic instructions on the other. One side of the A3 sheet contains a large isometric assembly drawing of the complete model and smaller illustrations on the other – two photographs of the resin parts, three diagrams of various sub-assemblies, and a camouflage drawing, quoting Humbrol paint references.

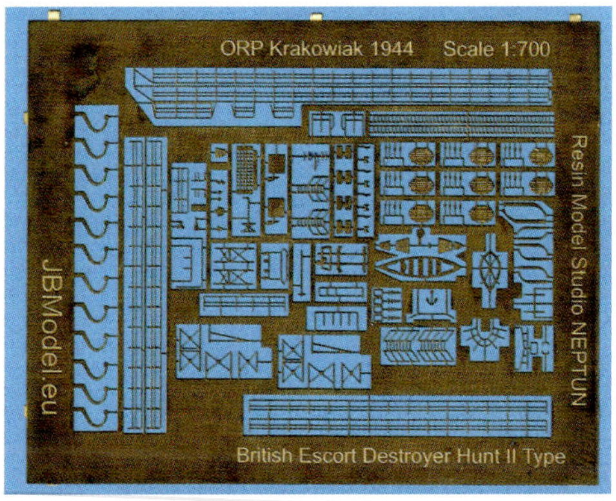

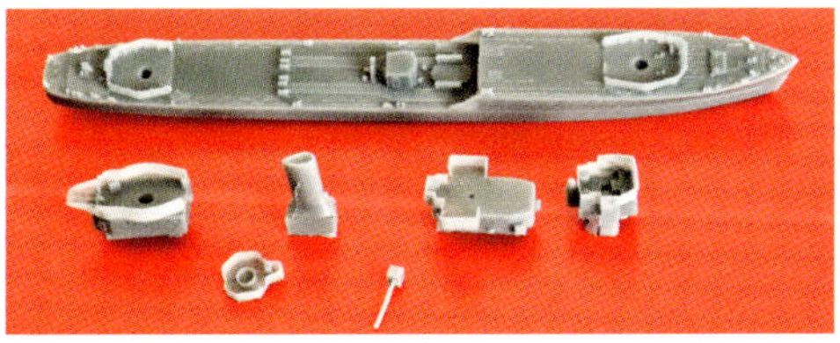

FINE WATERLINE SIG

1:700 scale

The IPMS Fine Waterline Special Interest Group have produced a 'semi-kit' of the Type 4 'Hunt' class destroyers *Brecon* and *Brissenden*. The kit included a waterline resin hull, the main superstructure and some smaller parts on a thin resin sheet. The instructions included a drawing of the vessel and suggestions as to suitable 'after-market' sources for some of the details, such as armament. Some scratch-building was required to complete the project.

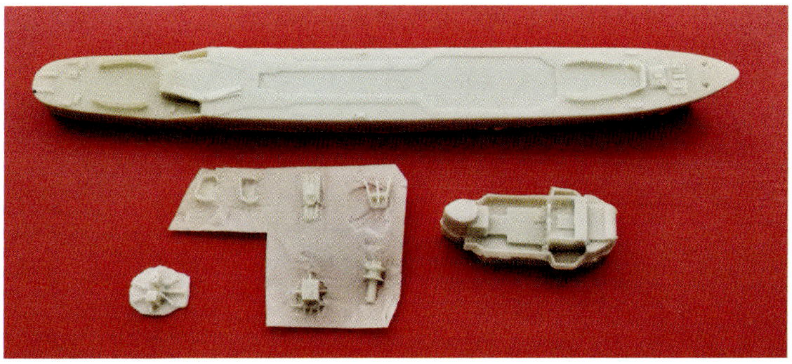

FLYHAWK

1:700 scale

Two plastic kits are available from Flyhawk – the *Wickes* class destroyer USS *Ward*, in US service, and HMS *Campbeltown*, as in 1942. Both kits can be modelled full-hull or waterline, a waterline plate being supplied to maintain the hull's shape if modelling this configuration. The models share a common hull moulding and a sprue containing the underwater parts, but the other sprues are very different.

There is a large sprue containing the deck and some of the smaller components

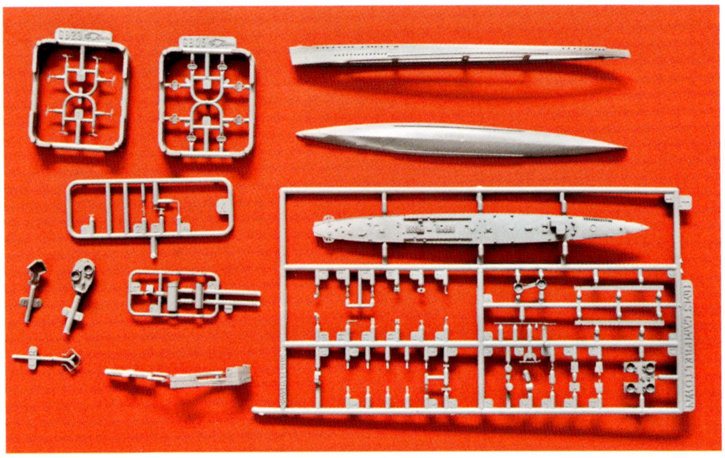

but the larger parts of the superstructure and funnels are provided on separate sprues. In the case of *Campbeltown*, these include some sprues that Flyhawk also market separately.

There are two sheets of etched brass, one of which includes a stand, with nameplate, for the full-hull model, and a decal sheet. In the case of *Campbeltown*, the etched brass sheet contains a number of commando figures to position around the ship. The instructions are provided on a long, double-sided sheet, beginning with component identity, followed by a number of assembly diagrams, and ending with colour details, the paints being specified from the Tamiya and Mr Hobby ranges, and the WEM Colourcoats range for *Campbeltown*.

These are both very finely moulded kits, and the photographs only show the parts from the kit of HMS *Campbeltown*.

HP MODELS

1:700 scale

The large range of resin kits from the German manufacturer HP Models includes six relevant models – a Type 2 and the Type 3 'Hunt' class destroyer, HMS *Eggesford*; the three 'S' class destroyers *Sabre*, *Saladin* and *Shikari*; and the ex-Dutch torpedo boat, HMS *Blade*. The box for the Type 2 'Hunt' class destroyer does not carry a particular ship's name, but included are basic colour details for the Polish *Krakowiak*.

They each comprise a resin waterline hull with one or two sheets of thin resin containing the other parts. In the case of the diminutive *Blade*, the waterline hull is moulded as part of a single, thin resin sheet. It is relatively easy to remove the larger parts, such as superstructure blocks, from the resin sheet, but removal of the smaller parts, without damage, is difficult.

Instructions are provided, in German, on two or three sheets of A4 paper, which

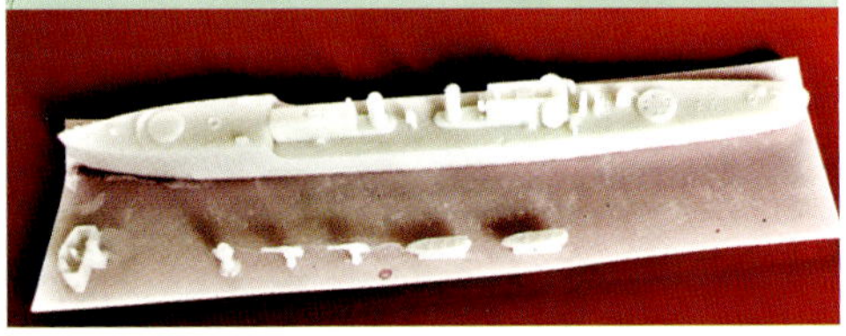

usually include a general arrangement drawing, an assembly diagram of the components and details of the masts and davits which are to be made from brass wire, supplied by the modeller.

IBG MODELS

1:700 scale

IBG Models market six 'Hunt' Type 2 destroyers, HM Ships *Badsworth* (1941), *Middleton* (1943) and *Zetland* (1942), plus three Polish vessels. The plastic kits are very similar, with just a few small variations, reflected by some of the smaller sprues supplied being different. The main differences lie with the details of camouflage schemes.

Each kit comprises a large sprue

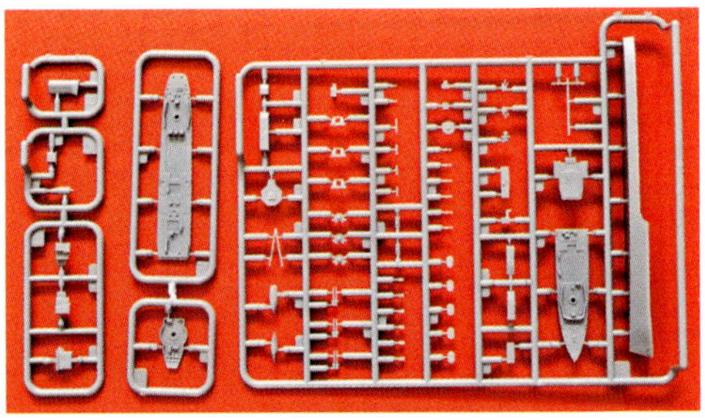

containing the one-piece waterline hull, foredeck, twin 4in guns, boats, carley floats, masts and other common details. It is in the five smaller sprues that the differences become apparent, the largest one containing the after deck, others containing the bridge, funnel, etc. The variations are small, such as different ready-use lockers and different sensors, reflecting the level of research carried out by the company. The plastic sprues are cleanly moulded with no flash.

The small sheet of etched brass, which includes railings, some of which are shaped to match the noticeable rise in the deck forward, are the same in each kit, as are the decals which include pennant numbers and ensigns for all six models.

The instructions are in a 6-page A4 booklet, with illustrations of the sprues and etched brass sheet on the front. Text is in both Polish and English. There are thirteen assembly diagrams, followed by a full-page perspective drawing illustrating the rigging, and a full-page camouflage drawing, with the paint colours being identified from the Hataka and LifeColor ranges.

NEPTUNIA

1:700 scale

This company mainly markets card models but this resin kit of the Type 1 'Hunt' class destroyer HMS *Belvoir*, is their first release in this medium. As well as a resin waterline hull, there is a bag of resin components for the superstructure, funnel, gun mountings, boats and other smaller details. An etched brass sheet is also supplied and a small decal sheet, which contains pennant numbers for HMS *Aldenham* as well as *Belvoir*. Finally there is a bag containing turned brass barrels for the 4in, 40mm and 20mm guns(!).

Instructions are provided on five sheets containing colour photographs of the assemblies. On the back sheet are camouflage patterns for both vessels as in 1942. On the front page are full size diagrams illustrating the mast assembly.

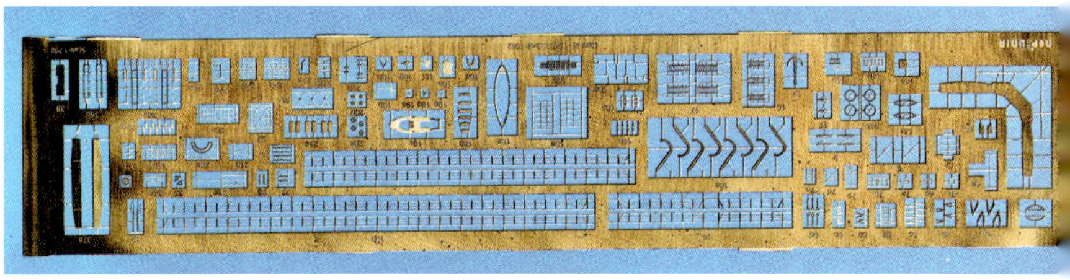

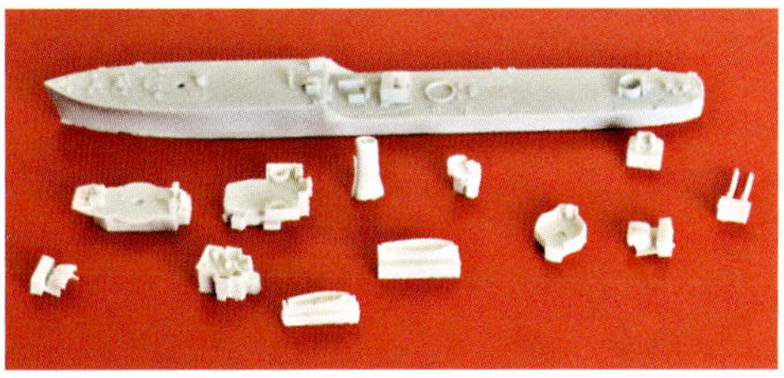

NIKO MODEL

1:700 scale

The resin waterline model of the 'Town' class destroyer HMS *Montgomery* from this Polish company is a very finely and cleanly moulded casting. In addition to the details moulded onto the hull, the kit includes two plastic bags of details, the upper parts of the superstructures, guns, boats, carley floats, torpedo tubes, cowl vents and fire control director. There is also a photo-etched sheet containing guardrails, propeller guards, gun shield, davits, ladders, masts and yardarms, and various antennas. The masts are produced by bending the etched material through 180° to increase thickness.

Instructions are supplied on two double-sided sheets of A4, the first page identifying both resin components and photo-etch parts. Pages 2 and 3 contain four assembly diagrams, with the back page containing colour details for the camouflage pattern carried in 1942. Paints are specified from the Colourcoats range.

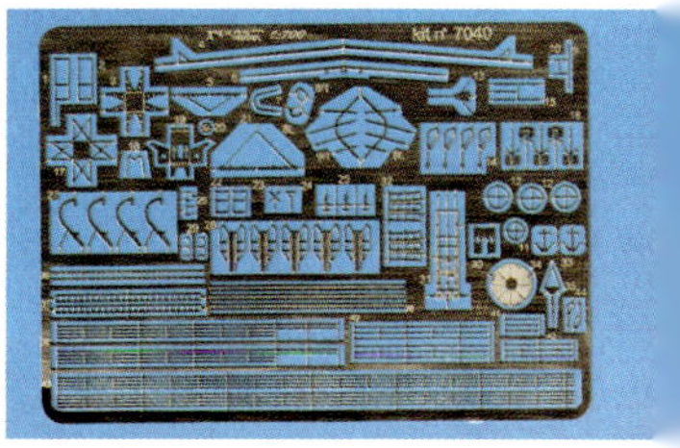

PAPER-LAB

1:700 scale

This model of the Type 1 'Hunt' class destroyer HMS *Liddesdale* as in 1942 was designed in Canada and is available via the Shapeways website. It is produced using 3D printing techniques and three parts are required to produce a complete model – Waterline Hull, Lower Hull and a 'Megasprue'. For the full-hull model, a stand is also available. Smaller sprues, containing a limited selection of parts, are also available for modellers who don't require the entire model. In addition to these parts available from Shapeways, Paper-Lab can also directly supply a set of instructions (pdf file), an etched brass sheet and decals. The model is translucent and Paper-Lab recommend priming with Tamiya Fine Surface Primer, after cleaning.

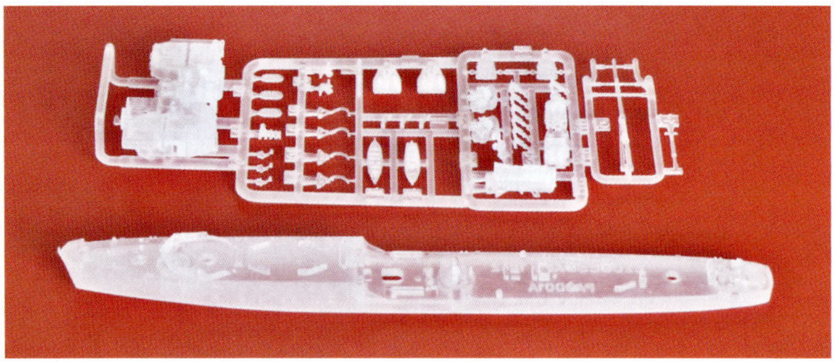

The parts are very fine and clean, no 'flash' as with many resin kits, and gun barrels and davits are particularly fine. The attention to detail is such that the davits are supplied in two different designs. The etched brass sheet includes railings and is clearly labelled. The instructions are clear and well illustrated in colour, and include a full colour scheme.

The level of detail possible with this manufacturing technique is probably higher than with others, and the model is highly recommended. The model is also available from Shapeways at 1:600 scale but Paper-Lab do not supply etched brass or decals at this scale.

TAMIYA

1:700 scale

This plastic kit of *Vampire* represents the destroyer after she transferred to the Royal Australian Navy in 1933. She was little changed from her original configuration and stayed this way throughout WWII.

The waterline hull is supplied in two halves, with a separate waterline plate and deck. The funnels are moulded in two halves, as is the bridge assembly, but smaller superstructure parts are moulded in one piece, as are the equipment pieces, such as guns and torpedo tubes. All mouldings are finely detailed and the masts are very fine. Small, rubber circles are provided in which to house the spigots of the main

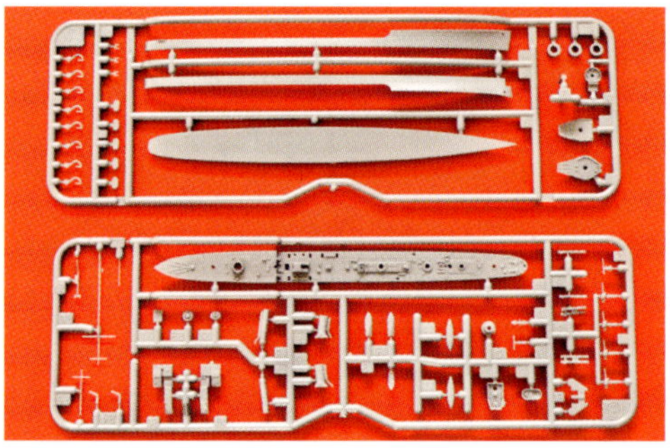

armament and torpedo tubes, to allow them to rotate after installation.

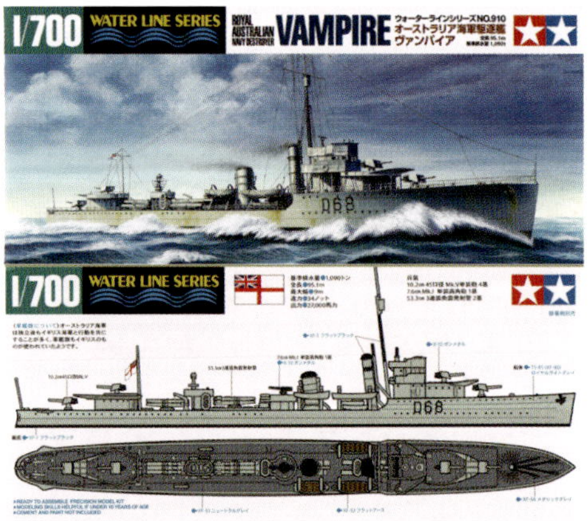

There is no etched brass but there is a decal sheet containing pennant numbers and a black band for the funnel. White ensigns are provided at two sizes, fully extended and as 'blown in the wind', on thin paper.

Instructions are supplied on two sides of a long piece of paper. On the first side are historical details and a drawing showing the colour scheme, the paints being identified from Tamiya's own range. This scheme is repeated on the bottom of the box. On the second side are six assembly diagrams, the first four showing the sub-assemblies, the next one assembly of the hull and major parts, and the final one illustrating the locations of the details.

WINGS, SHIPS, WHEELS

1:700 scale

The models of the Type 2 'Hunt' class destroyers *Badsworth* and *Fernie*, and the WAIR conversion HMS *Winchester*, come from Germany, packed in robust cardboard boxes. Originally very small boxes, just large enough to accommodate the kit parts, more recent production kits are in larger boxes. Inside is a waterline resin hull and a plastic bag containing the smaller components. These include the bridge, superstructure decks, main armament, boats, davits, carley floats, masts and AA guns. The instructions are contained on a single sided sheet of paper.

The masts are provided as very fine resin mouldings whereas the instructions provide dimensions for the use of brass rod. My instructions for *Badsworth* indicated that the barrels of the twin 4in gun were moulded separately and needed to be positioned in the turret, but the kit contained a single-piece moulding. These changes are due to improvements in moulding techniques which should make construction simpler for the modeller. In *Badsworth*, four 20mm guns are provided but these are not mentioned in the instructions (two should be installed on the bridge wings). They are included in the instructions for *Fernie*. These two models are similar but not identical.

A port profile provides details of a suitable camouflage scheme but no mention is made of deck colour (should be black-grey as used on the sides). No decals or etched brass are supplied.

AIRFIX

1:600 scale

This model is typical of their kits of the time (first released in 1961) – a full hull, split along the centreline, basic superstructure blocks moulded integrally with the deck, funnels moulded in two halves, a solid searchlight tower with the lattice moulded on the outer surfaces, and 'Aztec' steps. The model represents HMS *Campbeltown* when transferred to the Royal Navy in 1940, before any modifications were carried out.

The short historical and technical introduction is given in English, French and German. There are seven assembly diagrams, the last one showing the fitting of propellers, shafts and rudder. The colour diagram on the back page shows overall grey with a green deck, with yellow lifefloats, white boats and bronze anchors(!). There are no decals or etched brass.

A basically accurate kit but reflecting the moulding limitations of the time.

Airfix never produced a model of the

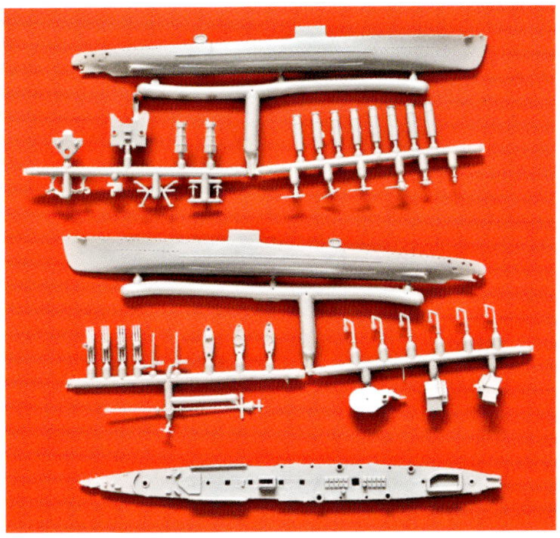

'Hunt' class, but the January and February 1971 issues of *Airfix Magazine* contained an article by Peter Hodges describing how to model one using the hull of HMS *Hotspur*, and adapting bits from other Airfix kits, with some scratchbuilding.

SKYTREX LTD

1:600 & 1:350 scale

These robust (and very heavy) white metal, waterline models are crude compared to today's plastic and resin kits, but basically accurate, and with the addition of after-market parts can be made quite acceptable. There is no etched brass or decal sheet, and the instructions are limited to a single sheet containing a line drawing for the 1:600 scale models and a black-and-white photograph of a completed model for the 1:350 scale models.

The 1:600 scale series includes a model of the Type 1 'Hunt' class destroyer *Berkeley*, the Type 2 'Hunt' *Middleton*, and three 'V&W' class destroyers, *Vivien*, *Versatile* and *Worcester*, in different configurations. Each model contains separate castings for the hull, bridge structure, funnel(s), mast, armament and boats, except that for *Worcester* where the boats are cast as part of the hull. The mast casting is representative of the tripod mast, but is solid, and the boats do not include davits.

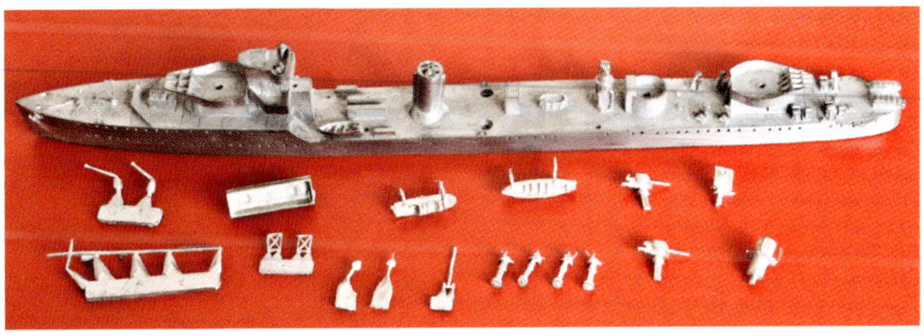

The 1:350 scale series includes four models of 'V&W' class destroyers in different configurations, as modified for operations in WWII. The four ships are HM Ships *Vanquisher*, *Versatile*, *Windsor* and *Winchester*.

The hull includes the bridge, funnel(s), major superstructures and depth charge throwers and rails. Cast separately are the gun platform (where applicable), bridge wing supports, armament, fire control director, mast, cranes and boats, with integral davits. There is some flash on the smaller components, but this is easily removed.

JSC

1:400 scale

This Polish company produce a range of waterline warship card models in A4 books.

Book 39 2/2016 contains three models, including ORP *Ślązak* (ex-HMS *Bedale*), a Type 2 'Hunt' class destroyer. On the front cover is an artist's illustration of the vessel at sea. Technical, historical and constructional details are included, in Polish at the front and in English at the back.

The English instructions for *Ślązak* occupy a page, and the coloured card components less than two pages. On the back is a small diagram showing the locations of the components.

Book 62 10/2002 contains two waterline models of the 'Town' class destroyer HMS *Campbeltown*. The first represents her as in 1941 and the second as in 1942, after modification to take part in the raid on St Nazaire, images of both models appearing on the front cover.

The details and instructions inside both the front and back cover are in Polish. Each model is contained on just one sheet of card, and there are no assembly diagrams but on the back cover are two diagrams showing the location of the components for each model. These also show the lengths of wire or brass rod required for parts such as davits and the mast.

Book 71 10/2003 includes a model of HMS *Vanity*. It has technical and model construction details in Polish at the front, followed by model constructional details in English. There are two sheets of coloured card, over three-quarters of the space being occupied by the components for *Vanity*. On the back cover are a general arrangement drawing showing the component locations, an overall assembly diagram, seven sub-assembly diagrams and dimensions for the mast and other lengths of rod/wire required to complete the model.

MIRAGE HOBBY

1:400 scale

This Polish company released five plastic kits of 'Town' class destroyers – HMS *Montgomery*, HNoMS *St Albans*, HMS *Campbeltown* and two US Navy ships, *Ward* and *Noa*. The first two were also released under the Airfix label, but the kits and reformatted instructions were the same. The kit of *Campbeltown*, representing her as in 1942, was released somewhat later than the others.

The kits come in flimsy boxes which open at the end. There are two large sprues, two smaller sprues and a base for the full-hull model. The hull is moulded in two halves, split along the centreline. One of the two smaller sprues is different between the two kits to allow for small variations. There is little flash but the mouldings are heavy, particularly noticeable in the lattice supports for the bridge wings and the funnel grilles. The mouldings of the mast and davits are finer. The kits do include separate mouldings for the bollards and fairleads, which have to be glued to the deck individually.

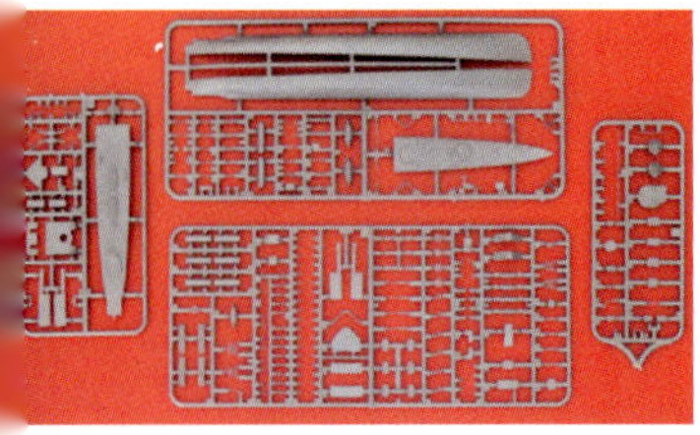

The kit of HMS *Campbeltown* comes in a more substantial box with a lid, similar to those used by Airfix for their versions of *Montgomery* and *St Albans*. In addition to the normal four sprues, there are two more supplying the revised funnels, gun platforms, etc, so there are numerous spare parts.

In all cases, the instructions are supplied in a 6-page, A5 booklet, the front page containing historical and technical details, both in Polish and English. Four pages are occupied with assembly diagrams, and the back page contains colour details, paints being specified from the Vallejo range. There is a small decal sheet containing pennant numbers (when applicable) and ensigns, but no etched brass.

ARMADA SCALE MODELS

1:350 scale

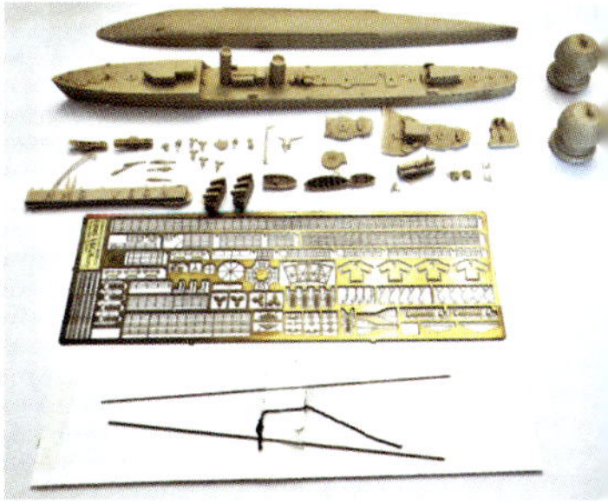

This resin kit is currently unavailable but The Resin Shipyard, Canada, intend to re-release it in the future. The model represents HMS *Vega* at the end of WWI, shortly after her completion, and the kit comprises a full hull, split at the waterline, two plastic bags of resin details, an etched brass sheet, two lengths of brass rod (different diameters), some brass chain and two resin pillars for mounting a full-hull model. Spares of the resin gun barrels are included.

The mouldings are well cast and clean, with only a limited amount of flash which can be removed quite easily. The fit of the parts is good, but some do lack detail when compared with modern 3D parts.

The instructions are supplied on six A4 sheets of paper, the first containing some detail of the original vessel, and the second identifying the components. The assembly diagrams are simple but clear, and the instructions include the dimensions for the masts, to be cut from the rod supplied. A simple colour scheme is included, paints being specified from the Humbrol range.

IRON SHIPWRIGHTS

1:350 scale

This American resin kit of the 'Hunt' class destroyer HMS *Middleton* is similar to others from this manufacturer and contains a cleanly moulded hull but the other resin parts have an excess of flash. In some cases, the flash is so extensive that it is difficult to identify the smaller parts. There is also a sheet of etched brass, containing railings, ladders, davits and other details, and two lengths of brass rod. A bonus with this kit, is a large, general purpose, decal sheet containing black and white numerals and letters in two different style.

As well as the extensive flash on many of the components, the larger superstructure parts frequently have resin rods (the remains of the 'pour') on the top surfaces which need to be removed with care so as not to damage the component. The kit includes a one-piece full hull, with a large 'pour' pedestal on its bottom, although the instructions show it split at the waterline. The ship's boats have too much beam and should be replaced with after-market parts to improve accuracy. Shields are not provided for the 20mm guns and the use of after-market parts for other items, such as the armament will certainly reduce preparation time and improve accuracy. Alternative parts are included, both for the bridge and the aft gun platform, to enable the model to be produced either as a Type 1 or a Type 2 vessel, but research is recommended, in both cases, to obtain maximum accuracy.

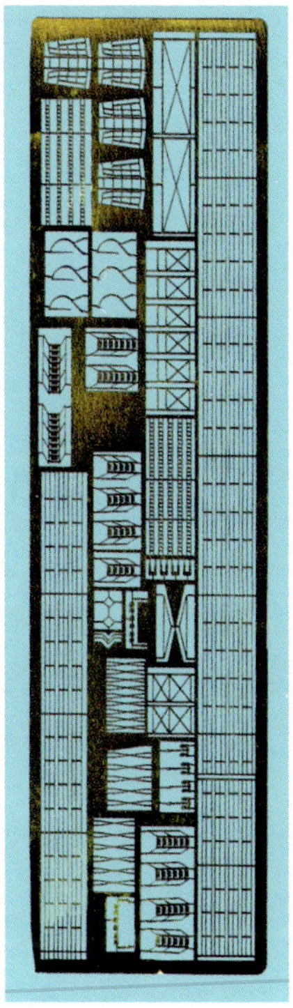

The instructions are rudimentary but do include basic camouflage profiles for four different destroyers; nevertheless, further research is required, the manufacturers recommending a suitable website. The Admiralty paint colours are identified as matching paints from the 'Dutch Boy' range. Two lengths of brass rod are included for the mast.

L'ARSENAL

1:350 scale

This French-manufactured full-hull, resin model of the Type 3 'Hunt' class destroyer HMS *Blean* comes in a substantial box. In addition to the hull, there are four plastic bags containing resin components, and one containing the two propellers, which appear to have been produced by 3D printing. The resin components all have substantial 'pours', particularly the hull.

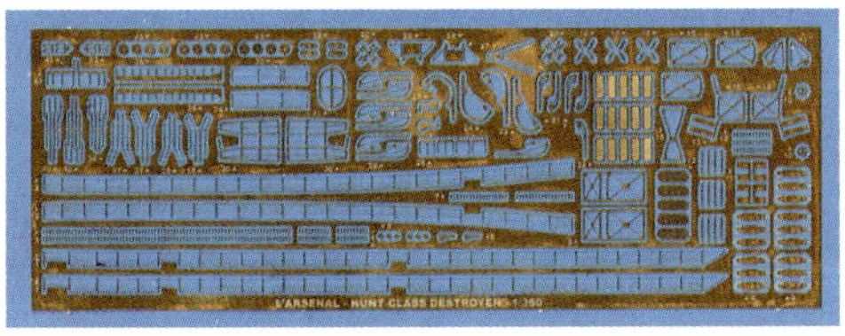

Further bags contain an etched brass sheet, tapered brass rod for the masts, brass gun barrels, and a decal sheet. This includes two sets of 'L and 0 – 9' in black, and four sets of larger numerals in white.

Extensive instructions are supplied on twelve A4 pages, colour being used to identify components. A colour diagram of a camouflage pattern is provided, but the colours are not identified and no paint references are given.

A high-quality model, requiring time, patience and skill to make the best of it.

SHOWCASE MODELS

1:350 scale

This plastic full-hull model representing HMS *Vendetta* as in service with the Royal Navy during WWI is manufactured in Australia. She was transferred to Australia shortly after the end of the war, with no changes apart from a lighter grey colour scheme and the addition of the pennant number D69, both schemes being shown in the instructions.

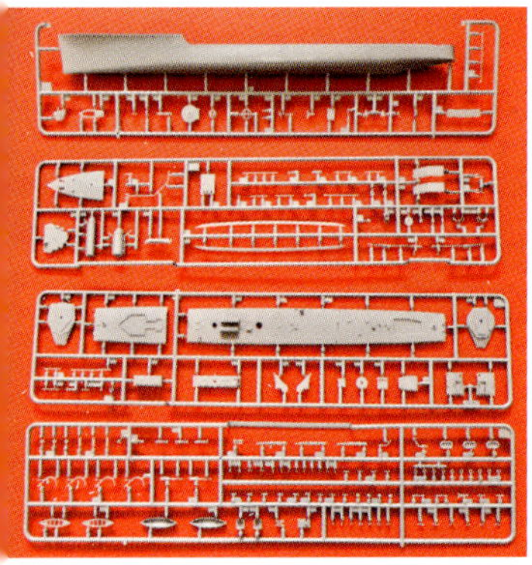

The components are supplied on five sprues, one of which is a duplicate. The hull is moulded in a single piece, with a separate four-part deck. The duplicated sprue includes the boats, davits, gun shields and other small details; the spares will be of use on other models. The sprues are cleanly moulded with no signs of flash. A separate sprue contains a display base.

There is an extensive decal sheet containing a full range of pennant numbers in black, white and white with black shading. The sheet also includes a range of British and Australian ensigns, and depth markings both in black and white. There are two etched brass sheets containing railings, ladders, anchor chain and other details, and a brass nameplate.

Instructions are provided in an 8-page booklet, with historical details on the front page and component identities on the second. This is followed by fourteen assembly diagrams. The colour schemes are contained on a separate page, and are produced full-size for the model, paint colours being identified from the Gunze range.

TOM'S MODELWORKS

1:350 scale

Sometime before 2010, the original proprietor of this American company released a resin model of HMS *Campbeltown*, as modified for the raid on St Nazaire in 1942. The model was withdrawn and unfortunately the current owner has no record of this model. In fact, he didn't know of its existence until the author contacted him.

The kit included a full hull, split at the waterline. With the cut-down superstructure required by the disguise, there were only a limited number of resin parts. The etched brass sheet included guardrails, propellers and propeller guards, rudder, depression rails for the gun mountings, anchor, funnel grids, bridge armour plating and ladders.

There were no decals and instructions were provided on three sides of A4. The first page included historical details and a plan and profile drawing of the vessel, indicating the locations of the parts. Page 2 gave details of sub-assemblies and page 3, detailed drawings of the arrangement of the 20mm guns. The instructions stated that the vessel was painted in 'Mountbatten Pink', and this is illustrated in the photograph of a completed model.

WHITE ENSIGN MODELS

1:350 scale

This resin kit of the 'Town' class destroyer HMS *Montgomery* was released by White Ensign Models (UK) in 2009 and includes a full-hull model, split at the waterline and a small plastic bag of resin parts for the superstructure, funnels, boats, main gun and ASW armament. A large etched brass sheet includes railings, ladders, davits, gun platforms, splinter matting, AA armament and details for the boats, masts, etc. There are also two lengths of brass wire for the masts.

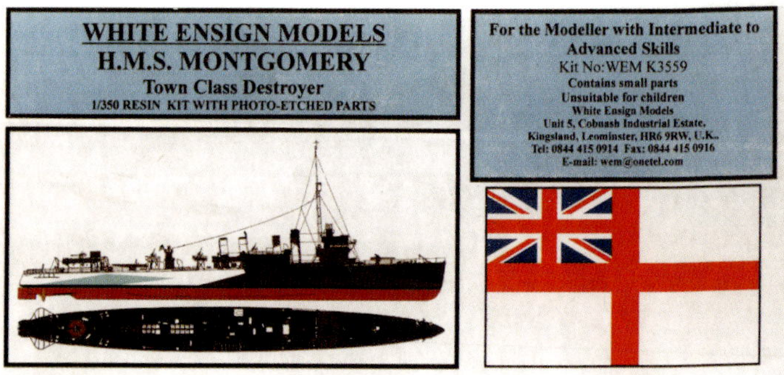

The resin parts are all cleanly moulded, with little flash. The instructions give technical details and some of the history of the destroyer, and clearly identify all the parts, both resin and etched brass. The assembly diagrams are clear and easy to follow. Some alternative etched brass parts are provided so that the destroyer can be modelled as the original USS *Wickes*, but some research will be required to accomplish this.

A camouflage scheme for *Montgomery* as in 1943 is provided, the paint colours being identified from WEM's own ColourCoats

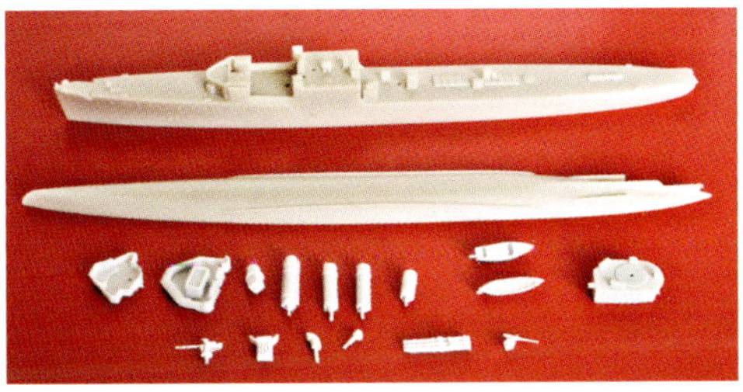

range, now available from Sovereign Hobbies. After WEM went into liquidation, manufacture of the model was taken over by Atlantic Models, the proprietor, Peter Hall, having produced the masters for WEM.

Some modellers may prefer to replace the brass AA armament with either resin mouldings or 3D printed parts to give them thickness.

REVELL

1:240 scale

This plastic model of HMS *Campbeltown* was first released in 1960 and has been re-released a number of times, the only change being the box and its artwork.

It is a full-hull model, with the hull in two parts, split along the centreline. Although flush decked, the deck is also supplied in two parts. Typical of models of this age, the mouldings are substantial, stanchions are included on the hull sides and the decks are scribed to represent wooden planking, even though the decks were actually metal. A stand is included for the full-hull model. The model represents the ship when first transferred to Great Britain, and includes hull numbers for her when in USN service. To represent the ship in Royal Navy service, a large number of modifications will be required. One point of interest is that the more detailed aspect of the lattice searchlight tower is on the inside faces, leaving the outside in a very poor condition.

Instructions are supplied in a 7-page A4 booklet containing 26 assembly diagrams. Paint colours are identified from Revell's own range, the colours of individual parts being identified by 'flags' scattered throughout the assembly diagrams.

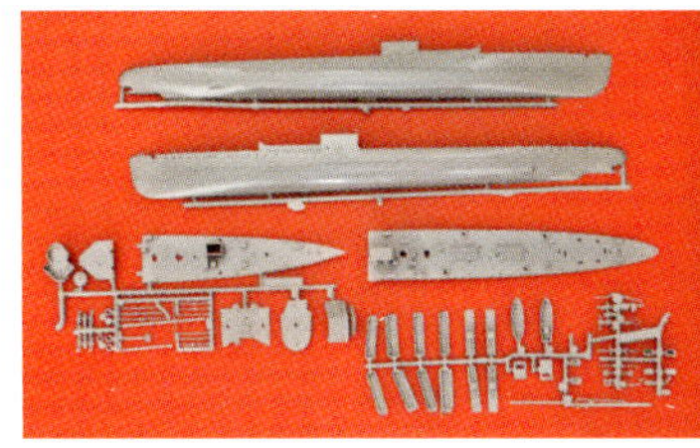

AJAKS

1:200 scale

This card model of the 'Hunt' Type 2 destroyer ORP *Kujawiak* (ex-HMS *Oakley*) is provided in an A4 book. The front cover has an artist's colour illustration of the vessel. Inside the front cover are technical, historical and constructional details of the vessel in Polish, and inside the back cover is a plan/profile drawing, showing the locations of the components.

There are just 1½ pages of assembly diagrams, illustrating the sub-assemblies, and 5½ pages of full-colour printed card containing the components for the vessel, plus 1½ pages containing the hull sections. The model can be built as a full-hull model if desired, and a stand is included.

This model is much simpler than the Neptunia or GPM ones, but provides an alternative camouflage scheme for a Type 2 'Hunt' class destroyer.

GPM

1:200 scale

The card model of a 'Hunt' Type 2 destroyer can be built as either HMS *Badsworth* or as HMS *Chiddingfold*, and is provided in a well-printed, high quality, A4 book. The front cover has a colour illustration of a completed model of *Badsworth* and small profiles of both ships, clearly showing different camouflage patterns. Inside the front cover are technical and historical details of both vessels, and inside the back cover are constructional details for the models, all in Polish.

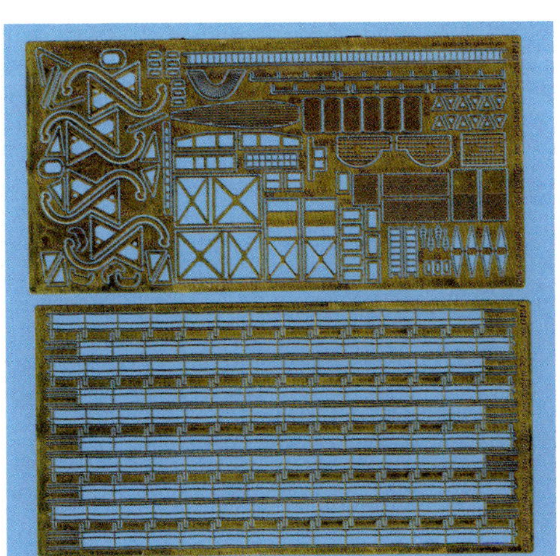

There are four pages of assembly diagrams, clearly illustrating the sub-assemblies, and two profile/plan drawings, one for each vessel. There are eleven pages of full-colour printed card containing the components for both vessels, plus two pages containing the hull sections. There is only one set of hull sections, so only one of the two vessels can be built. The model can be built as a full-hull model if desired, and a stand, with two sets of name plates, is provided.

To complement the model, two accessory sets are also available from GPM. There is a laser-cut set of thick card reproducing the frames for the hull. Also available is an etched brass sheet containing other details and hull railings.

The card model of HMS *Campbeltown* represents her as modified for the raid on St Nazaire, and is provided in a well-printed, high quality, A4 book. The front cover has a colour illustration of a completed model. Inside the front cover are technical, historical and assembly details of the vessel/model, in Polish.

The first page contains a profile/plan showing the locations of the parts, and details of the accessories available from GPM for this model. There are 4½ pages of assembly diagrams, clearly illustrating the sub-assemblies. There are four pages of full-colour printed card containing the components, plus two thinner pages containing the sections, which will require reinforcing with card before use. The model can be built as a full-hull model if desired, but no stand is provided.

To complement the model, three accessory sets are also available from GPM. There is a laser-cut set, two sheets of thick card reproducing the frames for the hull, and two thinner sheets, one in grey, providing small details. Also available is an etched brass sheet containing other details, but not hull railings. Finally, there is a set of turned brass gun barrels, including 102mm (4in) and 20mm mountings.

NEPTUNIA 1:200 scale

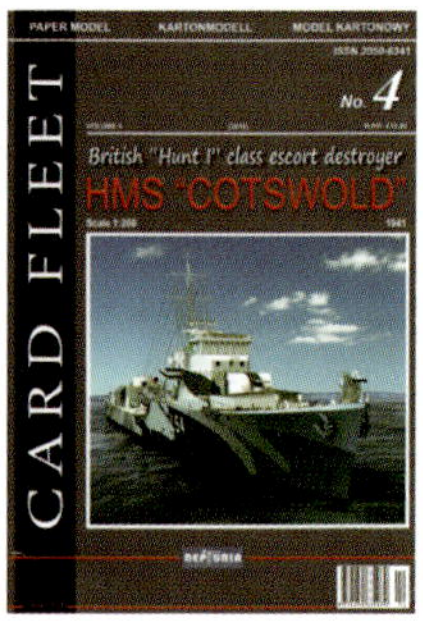

This card model of HMS *Cotswold*, a Type 1 'Hunt' class destroyer, is provided in a well-printed, high-quality, 28-page, A4 book. The front cover has a colour illustration of a completed model. The first two pages include technical, historical and assembly details of the vessel/model, in the English language. These are repeated on the back two pages in Polish, reflecting the popularity of card modelling in that country.

There are eight pages of assembly diagrams, clearly illustrating the sub-assemblies. There are eight pages of full-colour printed card containing the components, plus two pages containing the sections and other internal constructional parts. In the centre are two double-page spreads showing a perspective drawing of the finished model, and a plan/profile drawing, identifying the location of the components. The model can be built as a full-hull model if desired and a stand is included.

To complement the model, four accessory sets are also available. There is a laser-cut set, three sheets of card reproducing the frames for the hull, funnel and

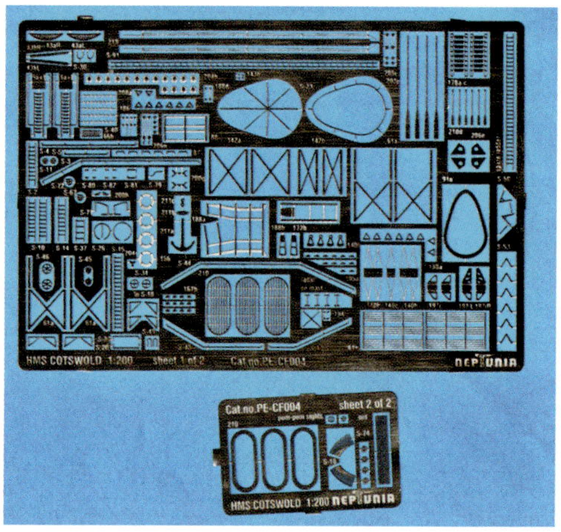

other larger superstructure parts, and parts for the display base. Also available are two etched brass sheets containing details for the funnel, fire-control director aerials, supports for the overhanging parts of the superstructure, boat and carley float details and ladders, but not hull railings. Finally, there is a set of brass rod for the mast and a set of turned brass gun barrels, including 102mm (4in), 40mm, 20mm and 0.5in mountings.

DEANS MARINE 1:96 scale

Intended primarily for radio control operation, a plated fibreglass hull forms the base for this model. Decks and superstructure are in 1mm laser-cut plastic sheet with 0.5mm sheet for the two main structures. Over 150 cast metal and cast plastic items, along with vacforming for all gun shield, gun cabs, ship's boats are provided.

An etched brass sheet containing the stanchions is included, and the kit is complete with all running hardware: *ie*, prop tubes, prop shafts in stainless steel, rudder, tiller arm etc. The instructions are supported on a CD showing various stages in the construction.

ACCESSORIES

ETCHED BRASS DETAIL SETS

Guardrails are available from a large number of manufacturers, at different scales. The main manufacturers/suppliers in the UK are Atlantic Models (1:700, 1:600 and 1:350) and Starling Models (1:700), in France L'Arsenal (1:700, 1:600, 1:400, 1:350 and 1:200) and in the USA Tom's Modelworks (1:1250, 1:700, 1:600, 1:400 and 1:350) and Gold Medal Models (1:700, 1:600, 1:400, 1:350 and 1:200). These are suitable for any of the models reviewed.

STARLING MODELS

1:700 scale

This sheet, STM13, is for use with a number of different WWII Royal Navy Destroyers, including the 'V&W' class. The parts supplied include a funnel platform, four gun shields, searchlight tower, depth charge racks, a variety of platform supports, funnel grids and some supports for a variety of AA gun platforms.

In addition to the parts specifically for 'Tribal' class, 'O' class and 'E' class destroyers, there some generic parts such as davits, 20mm Oerlikon guns and railings. The two pages of instructions clearly identify which parts are intended for which classes and give some assembly photographs of antennas, towers and platforms. A very useful set.

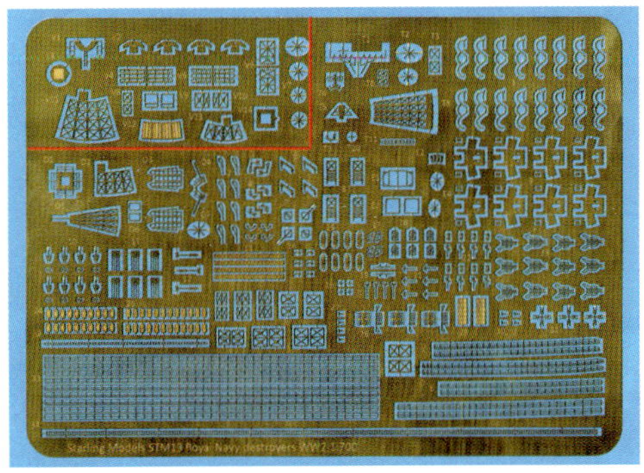

WHITE ENSIGN MODELS

1:700, 1:600 & 1:400 scale

Sheet PE791 (V&W class destroyers) is for use in conjunction with the Tamiya kit (1:700 scale) of HMS *Vampire*. It includes a large number of parts which permit other vessels to be built – the aft pom-pom platform of HMS *Wallace* is specifically mentioned, as are the 4in gun spray shields for a WAIR conversion. It is necessary to research the specific vessel to be modelled, so as to identify, for example, which of the bridge wing variants and bridge wing supports, are applicable. Many of the parts, for example the foremast, ship's boat and depth charge details, are applicable to many vessels.

Instructions are provided on three double-sided sheets of A4, containing the component identities on the front sheet, and clear location and assembly drawings of the components.

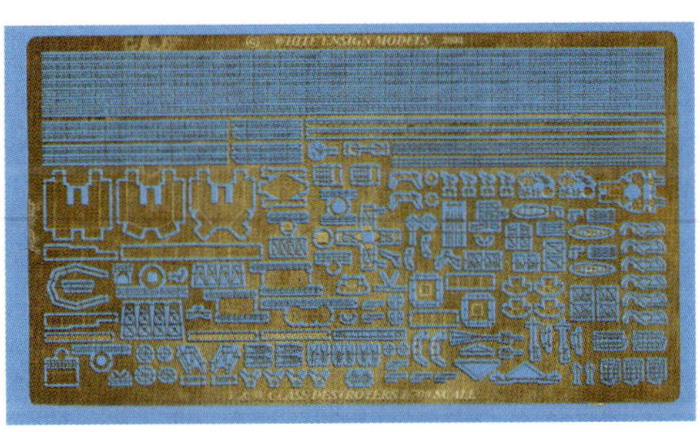

Sheet PE630 (WWII British destroyers & escorts Set 1) is for use with a number of different Airfix kits (1:600 scale) including HMS *Campbeltown*. There are just fourteen parts for *Campbeltown*, including alternative propeller guards of both British and American type. Forecastle railings, boat skids and davits, depth charge rails and a 3in Mk 14 gun are also included.

Instructions are provided on three double-sided sheets of A4, containing the component identities on the front sheet, with assembly drawings of the components for *Campbeltown* on pages 4 and 5.

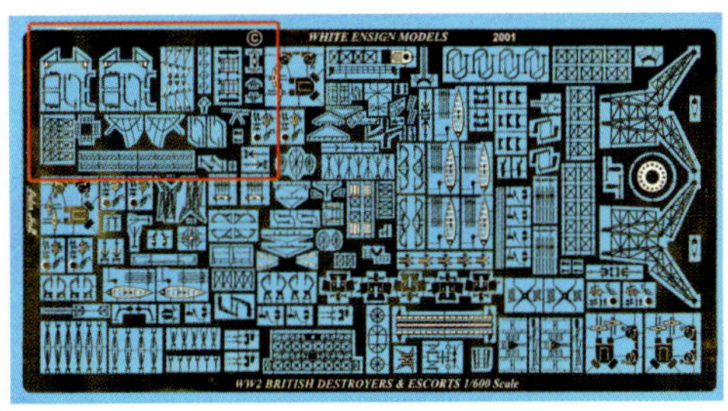

Sheet PE4015 covers USN and RN flush-deck destroyers and is for use in conjunction with the many different Mirage and Airfix kits (1:400 scale) available of this class. It was not designed for use with the Mirage kit of HMS *Campbeltown* as in 1942, but some parts will be of use. A range of different railing configurations are supplied, including ones with nets or canvas dodgers, as well as open ones. Alternative railings are also supplied for the bridge roofs of HMS *St Albans* and HMS *Montgomery*.

Some parts are identified as being specific to USN or RN configurations, and some as specific to individual vessels. 20mm Oerlikon guns, 0.5in machine guns and depth charge throwers are included, but many modellers will want to replace these with either resin or 3D parts, to provide thickness.

Instructions are provided on five sides of A4, containing the component identities on the front sheet, with assembly drawings and location on the others, clearly identifying which configuration, USN or RN, or vessel they apply to.

GOLD MEDAL MODELS

1:400 & 1:240 scale

This sheet is for use in conjunction with the many different Mirage and Airfix kits available of 'Town' class destroyers at 1:400 scale, in particular that of USS *Ward*. It was not designed for use with the Mirage kit of HMS *Campbeltown* as in 1942, but some parts will be of use. A range of different railing configurations are supplied, including ones with canvas covers, as well as open ones. The main deck railings do include lower sections to permit rotation of the torpedo tubes.

Gun shields are provided for the 4in guns and the 20mm Oerlikon guns. Alternative depth charge roller racks of different lengths are provided, depending on which particular vessel is being modelled. With particular reference to USS *Ward*, a figure of the captain is also included. The searchlight tower of USN vessels is provided, together with mast yardarms, doubled to increase thickness, to replace the kit parts.

Instructions are provided on two sides, including a profile drawing of a 'typical' destroyer.

The 1:240 scale, thick brass sheet includes parts for two Revell kits, the USS *Buckley* and the USS *Ward*. The parts for USS *Ward* are equally suitable for HMS *Campbeltown* when first transferred to Great Britain, but not for a model of her when in RN service, after modifications. The double-sided instruction page clearly identifies which parts are applicable to each model. Those particularly applicable to the '4-pipers' are searchlight tower, depth charge roller racks, 4in gun details, funnel cap grilles, boat davits, DF antenna, bridge windows, rafts and boat oars, ship's wheel and mast yardarms. If the modeller wishes to model HMS *Campbeltown* later in her career, only a limited number of parts, including guardwires, ladders and doors, will be of use.

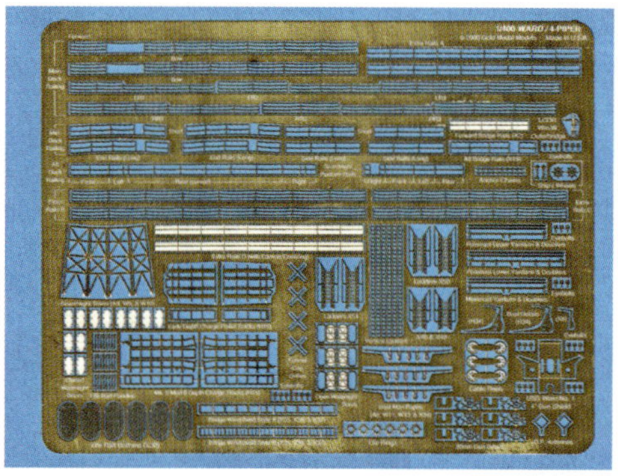

FINE MOLDS

1:700 scale

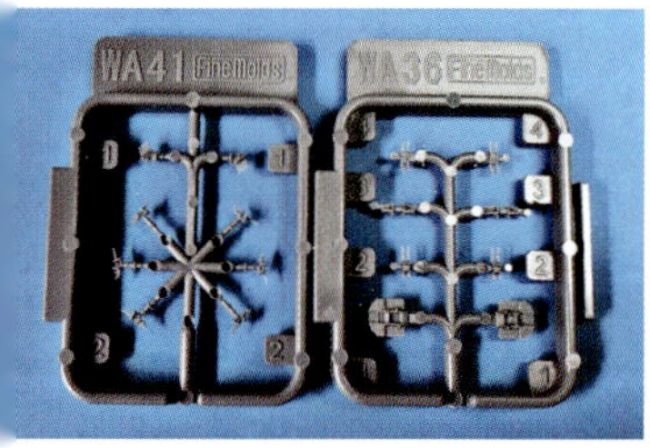

This Japanese company produces a range of very fine plastic accessories. Each pack contains four rectangular sprues with the components in the centre. Each sprue for the 20mm guns contains six mountings (plus two quad 0.5in mountings). Each quad pom-pom mountings comprises four separate parts, two mountings being included on each sprue. The boat davits include rope blocks and there are four on each sprue. Shields are not included for the 20mm guns, but a sheet of etched brass containing 105 shields is available from Starling Models (STM42).

These accessories are much finer than found in many kits and will enhance the general fidelity of the model.

FLYHAWK MODEL

1:700 scale

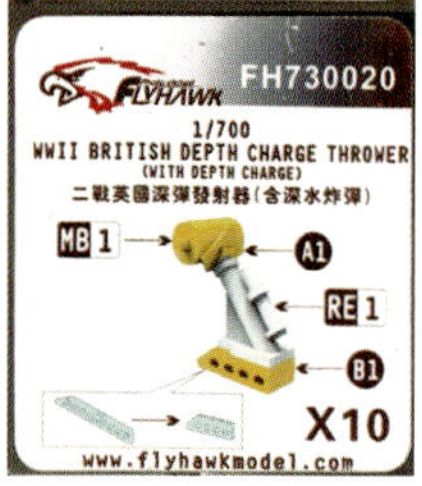

Many of the Flyhawk models include rectangular sprues containing small, common parts. Some of these are available separately: FH1500 RN AA Weapons contains four sprues, each including two quadruple 40mm (2pdr) pom-pom mountings, two quadruple 0.5in mountings and one 20mm mounting; FH1501 RN Searchlights contains two sprues, each containing four large and six small searchlights; FH1502 RN Deck Equipment contains two sprues, each containing four winches and six paravanes; FH1503 RN Life Rafts contains two sprues, each containing four carley floats; FH1504 RN Oerlikon 20mm contains four sprues, each containing eight mountings; FH1505 RN Ship's Boats contains two sprues, each containing two 27ft whalers, two 25ft fast motor boats, two 16ft fast motor boats and one 32ft motor cutter. The 20mm guns do not include shields, but Flyhawk also

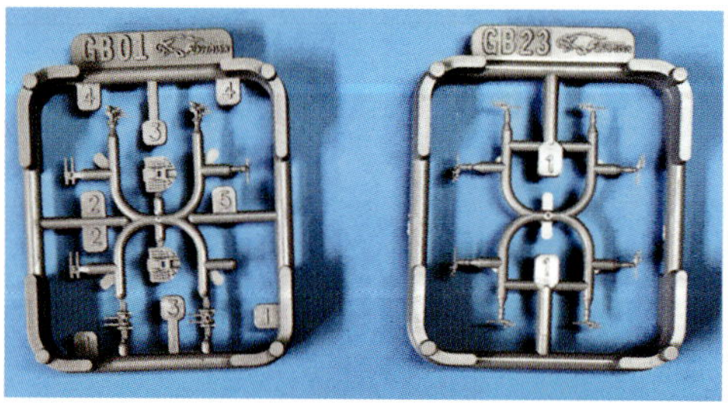

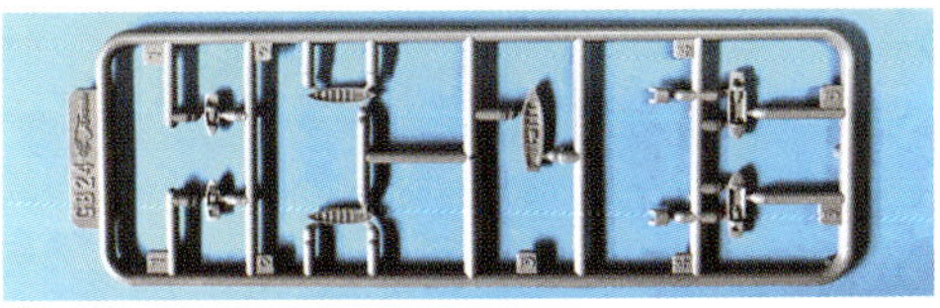

supply FH1500s and FH1504s which include etched brass. Alternatively, a sheet of etched brass, containing 105 shields for the 20mm Oerlikon guns, is available from Starling Models (STM42).

Also available is FH730001 which contains four twin CPXIX mountings for 4.7in Mk XII guns and FH730002 which contains four twin Mk XIX mountings for 4in Mk XVI guns. These each comprise plastic turrets, etched brass and turned brass barrels. FH730020 contains ten depth charge throwers, which each comprise an etched brass base, a resin upstand and a turned brass depth charge. These three items are very detailed and intended for modellers with above average skills – and very good eyesight!

L'ARSENAL 1:700 scale

Among other accessories produced by this French company is a set of Royal Navy Speedboats (AC 700 37). Each packet contains two of each of the following: 14ft dinghy, 16ft motor dinghy, 25ft motor boat, 27ft whaler, 32ft life cutter, 35ft motor boat and 36ft life cutter. Each detailed resin boat is finely detailed, with no flash, but needs to be removed from a substantial size sprue.

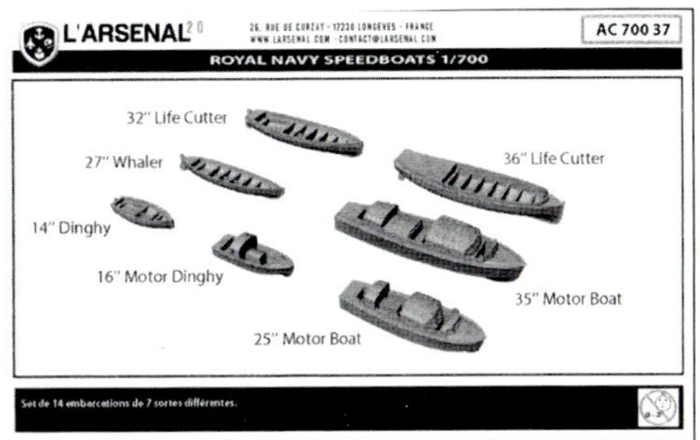

MASTER MODEL 1:700 and 1:350 scale

For those who want to improve their 'brass rod' masts, this Polish company produce two sets of masts and two sets of yardarms, both at 1:700 and 1:350 scale. Each set includes different lengths and diameters of brass rod, tapered at the end – one end for the masts and both ends for the yardarms.

The masts can be cut to length by removing the untapered end, but the modeller will need to select the closest length for the yardarms – small detail but it can be quite noticeable, particularly at 1:350 scale.

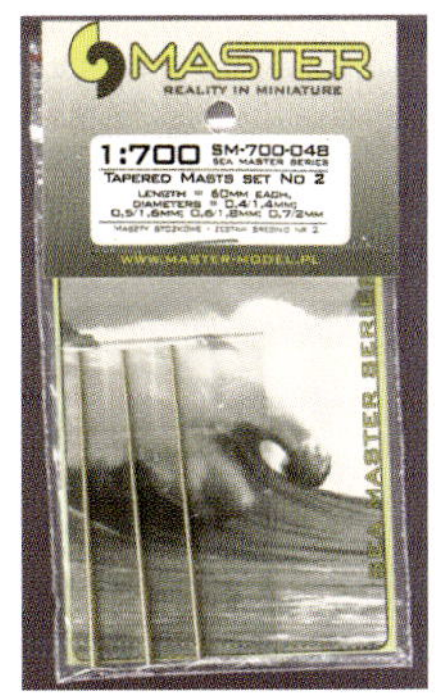

MICRO MASTER 1:700, 1:600, 1:400, 1:350 & 1:200 scale

This company from New Zealand initially sold their 3D printed products via the Shapeways website, but have recently obtained their own manufacturing capability and are now selling directly from their own website, although the earlier products are still available from Shapeways. Production facilities are limited in size but the quality and detail is still high, just requiring the modeller to carry out a little more work when removing the component from the printing base. Taking full advantage of 3D printing capabilities, the components are available at a wide range of scales.

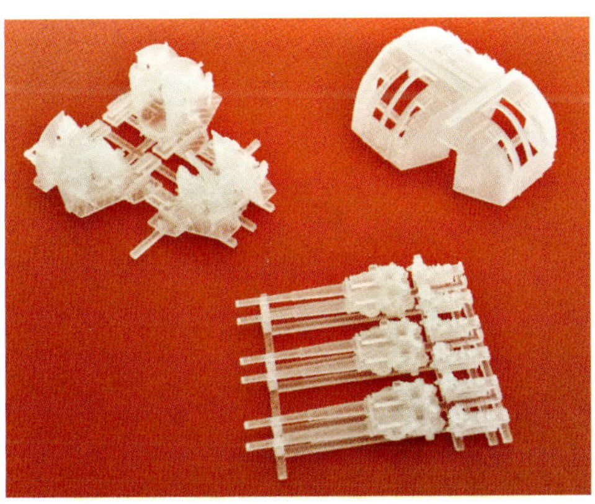

Although Micro Master specialise in components for Royal Navy ships, they also produce accessories for the Kriegsmarine, the French Navy, the US Navy, and even a few for the Greek Navy. Their website contains much technical information on the piece of equipment being modelled.

Items available at 1:700 scale which are particularly relevant to the models reviewed in this book include twin 4in gun mounting, quad 0.5in gun mounting, single 20mm gun mounting (includes integral shield), 25ft motor cutter and fast motor boat, 27ft whaler, various sizes of carley float, and depth charge thrower and rail. The majority of these are also available at larger scales.

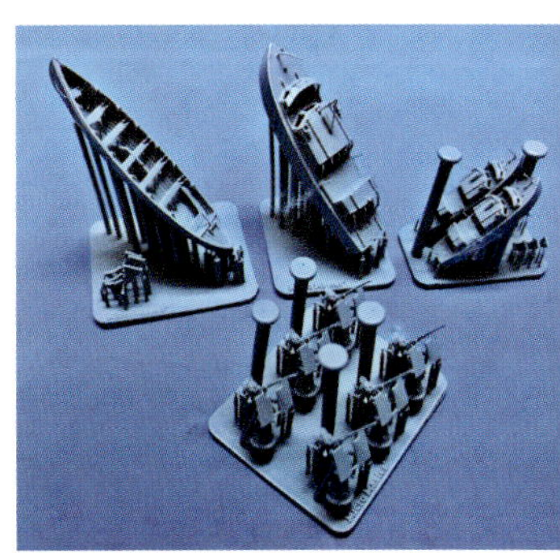

BLACK CAT MODELS 1:350 scale

This French company produce an extensive range of 3D printed accessories, not only for the Royal Navy, but also for the Kriegsmarine and US Navy. The range includes gun armament, fire directors, torpedo tubes, searchlights, boats,

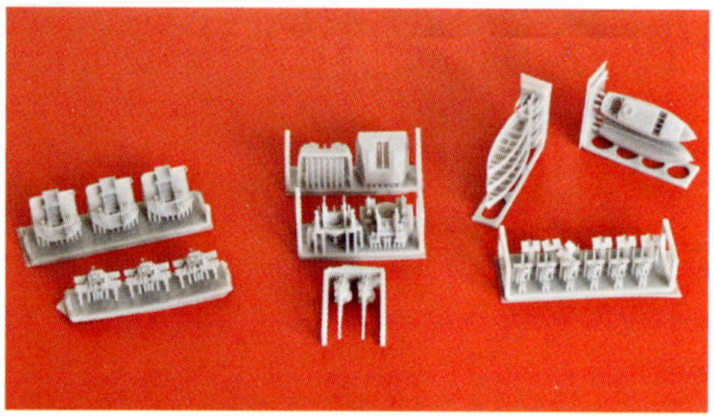

carley floats, deck equipment, deck lockers and cowl vents. Of particular interest are the twin 4in gun mountings, single 20mm Oerlikon guns, depth charge throwers, depth charge rails, Hedgehog mortars, 27ft whaler and 25ft cutter.

All are very detailed and supplied in small, plastic cases, for protection. Just requiring a wash to remove any residue and priming, the fittings are ready for painting.

NIKO MODELS

1:700 and 1:400 scale

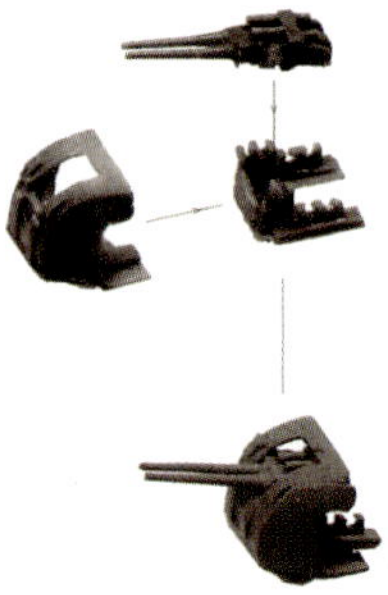

This Polish company produce a range of resin accessories, including the twin 4in gun mounting (5 per pack), quadruple 40mm (2pdr) pom-pom (2 per pack) and quadruple 0.5in Vickers mounting (5 per pack) at both scales. These are cleanly moulded and will improve many kits.

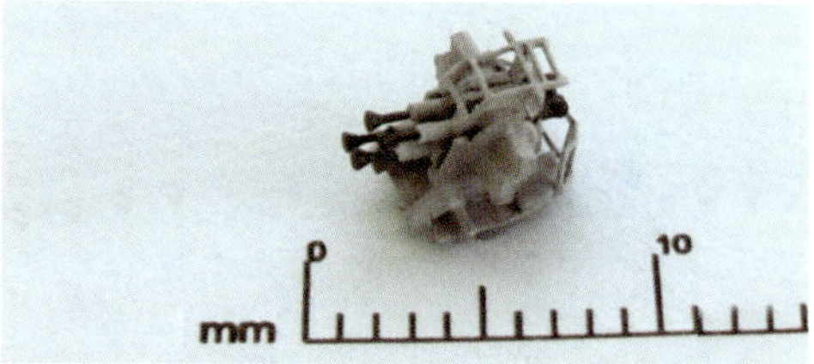

INFINI MODEL

1:350 scale

Each packet of 20mm Oerlikon Cannon Mk IV Mounts (Royal Navy), IMP-35011R1, from China, contains twenty-five mounts and each mount consists of a brass gun barrel, pedestal and magazine, with the shield, supports and sight provided on a sheet of etched brass.

IMP-35048R1 contains six Royal Navy Vickers 0.50cal quad mounts, each consisting of a brass turntable, a milled central support, four barrels, with the sights, handwheels and other details on a sheet of etched brass.

These are detailed products for the modeller with above average handling skills!

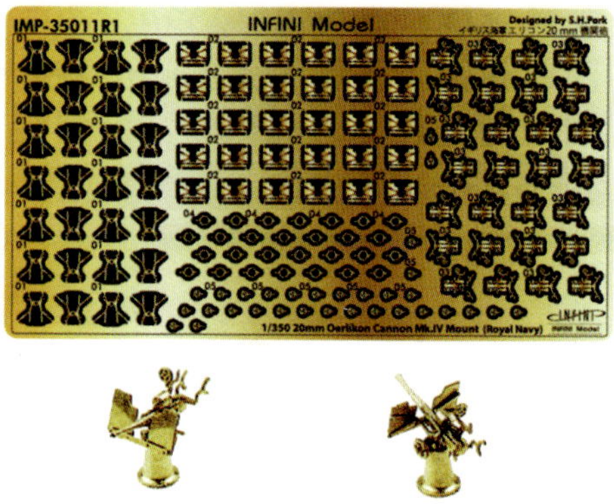

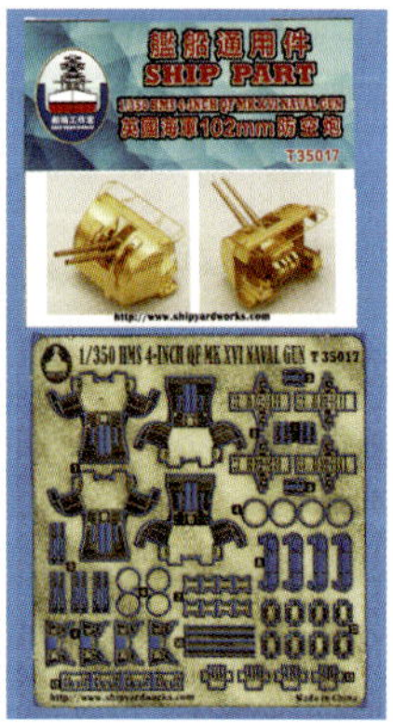

SHIPYARDWORKS

1:350 scale

Another product from China aimed at more skilled modellers. Each packet of the 4in QF Mk XVI naval gun (T35017) contains an etched brass sheet for four mountings and eight brass barrels. Construction begins with the trunnion supports and the shield is curved and added after. The etched brass sheet is relief-etched on both sides to provide additional detail – a high quality product.

GPM

1:200 scale

In addition to producing card models and accessories for them, the Polish company GPM also produce a number of accessories for use with other manufacturers' models. These include 20mm Oerlikon and 40mm (2pdr) pom-pom guns.

Each of the two sheets for the 20mm Oerlikon guns contain four mountings. They are grey in colour and require the pedestal to be produced by curving the part supplied into a circle. The 40mm pom-pom set also includes two sheets, but each sheet includes just one mounting, again pre-coloured grey. Both mountings are intended for use with the appropriate barrels available from the same manufacturer.

GPM also produce turned metal barrels for use with a range of other card models, including HMS *Campbeltown* and HMS *Vega*.

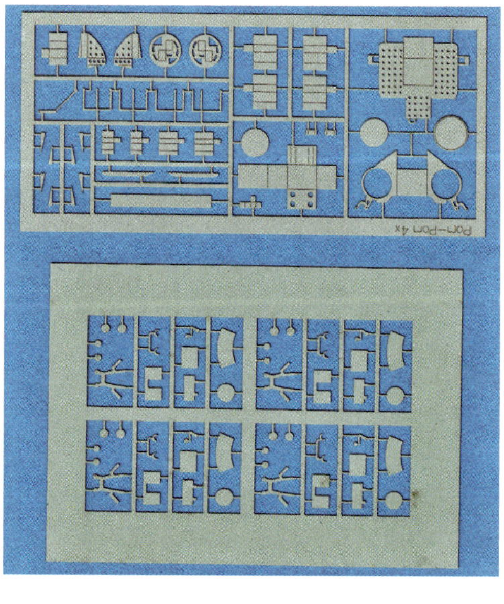

Modelmakers' Showcase

PAPER-LAB *LIDDESDALE* 1:700 scale

By DAVE EYLES

Being a 3D printed model, a great amount of detail is included on each part, resulting in only a few pieces to be assembled. Working with translucent material can be very difficult when locating the smaller parts, hence the manufacturer's suggestion to prime the parts before assembly. The fit of the parts was excellent. AK Interactive and Hataka paints were used, both being highly suited to use by an airbrush.

AJM MODELS ***MALCOLM*** AND WHITE ENSIGN MODELS ***MONTGOMERY*** 1:350 scale

By DAVE EYLES

During the build of these two models, some of the small details (small calibre gun mountings and depth charge throwers on both *Montgomery* and *Malcolm*, and the Hedgehog mortar on *Malcolm*) were replaced by 3D printed parts from Black Cat Models. This was particularly noticeable when replacing the etched brass 20mm Oerlikon guns on *Montgomery*, giving a three-dimensional appearance rather than a flat one.

The railing supplied with *Malcolm* did not include a continuous rail at the bottom, but had individual stanchion points for attaching to the model, and so was replaced. Paints used were a combination of ColourCoats, Vallejo, LifeColor, Hataka and AK Interactive.

G95

AIRFIX *CAMPBELTOWN* 1:600 scale

By DAVE WOOLEY

These two models, both made from the same kit, represent *Campbeltown* as first delivered (before any modifications) and as modified for the raid on St Nazaire. Dave used WEM PE on both models, with some scratch building and a few 3D printed parts.

NEPTUNIA *COTSWOLD* 1:200 scale

By MARIUSZ JANISZEWSKI

Building card models presents substantially different challenges to building the more popular resin and plastic models. The 'kits' are significantly lower cost, the tools required are basic (a pair of scissors, a knife and a straight edge will cover most requirements) and no paint is needed.

This sample of a 'test' model, built by Marius Janiszewski, shows how effective the outcome can be. The limitations of card as a modelling material can be difficult to overcome, but with care and patience, and a little thought, the results are impressive.

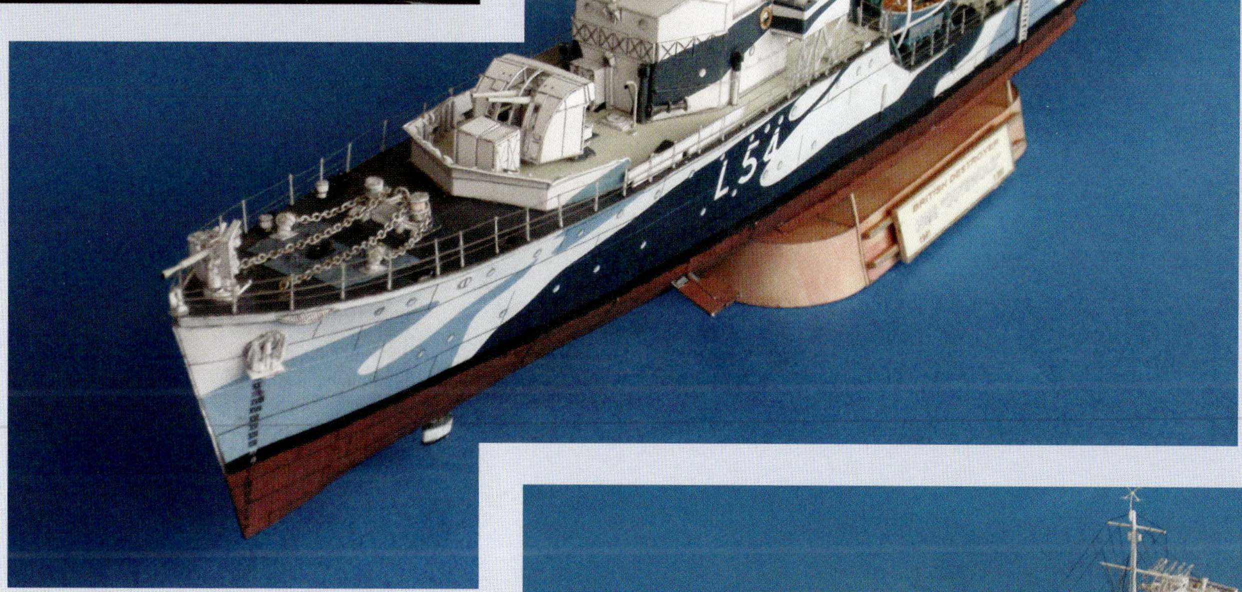

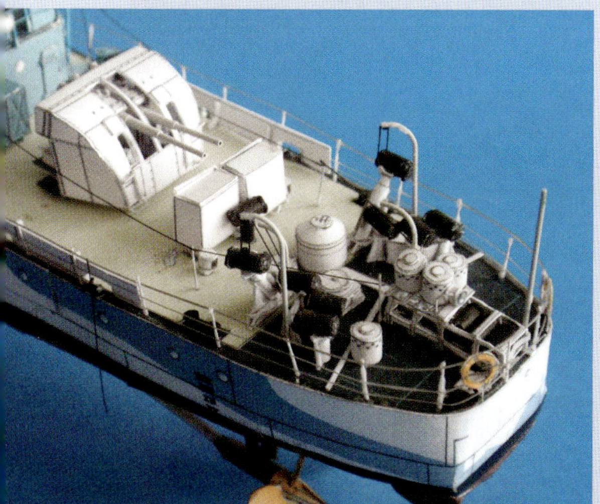

SCRATCH-BUILT *HAMBLEDON* 1:72 scale

By IAN McFARLANE

This model is radio-controlled, using electric motors for propulsion. Active stabilisers are fitted. The hull is constructed from wood, the keel and frames being laser-cut from 4mm ply. Planking is in 2mm lime, and the inside lined with glass fibre tissue. Decks are from 0.5mm plasticard. The majority of the parts were built from scratch, but some of the more detailed items (such as the boats and armament) were purchased from either MicroMaster (3D printed parts) or Great Little Ships.

Ian used the Neptunia card model *Cotswold* for many details and also obtained plans of *Mendip* from the National Maritime Museum, now part of Royal Museums Greenwich.

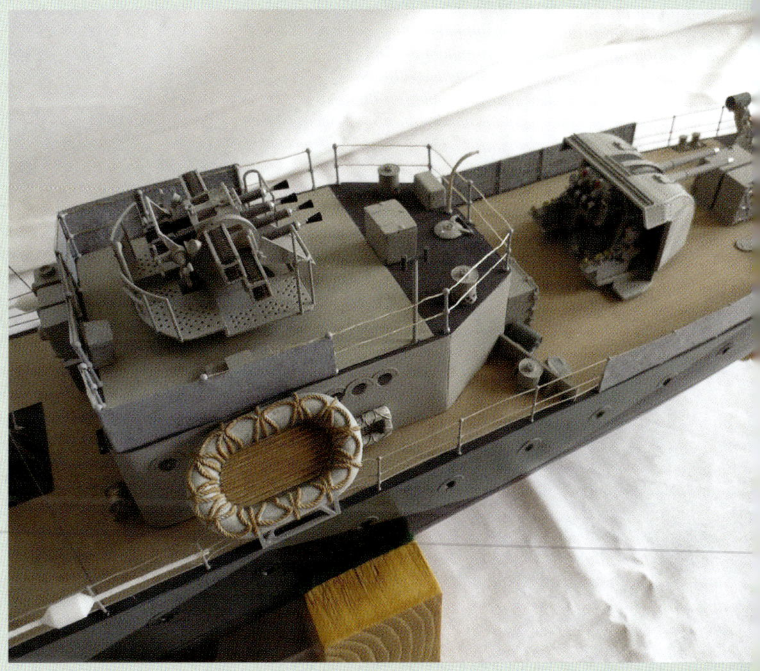

CHOROSKY MODELBUD *OAKLEY* AND WSW *ROXBOROUGH* 1:700 scale

By PETER FULGONEY

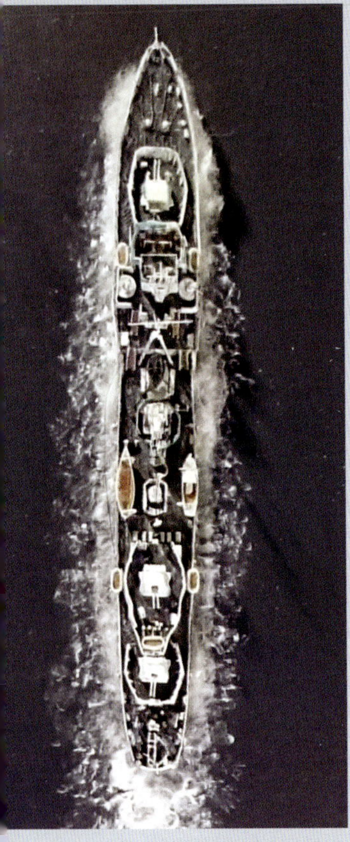

The Chorosky Modelbud 'Hunt' class Type 2 resin model kit includes a comprehensive set of parts, including Sea Master gun barrels, metal masts, decals and a good number of small parts, including a good photo-etch selection, all to enable the modeller to build a complete representation of this class of ship.

The resin hull was subject to 'hogging' but it was glued and weighed down into a flat position. There was also some sanding and fitting to do, but the only real drawback was the general identification and placing of parts, so the modeller will need good references and a clear idea as to which ship is to be portrayed.

Peter's build depicts *Oakley* in action, painted in the 'western approaches' camouflage scheme. The water effect is artist's watercolour paper painted dark sea green and with three coats of Johnson's clear gloss finish or similar. Added to this is AK Water Gel, and Daler Rowney texture paste. The rigging is Van der Rossen 'rig that thing', some stretched sprue, and Albion Alloys 0.01mm metal rod.

When building a smaller ship – and at 1:700 scale the US four-stack destroyer is a miniscule subject – it is a good idea to consider it as part of a story, as then a broader scenario may be envisaged. With some net curtain, 3D printed sailors and ship's boats, the sunken ship rescue begins to become much more animated than just the ship by itself. The WSW kit of *Borie* has been updated and converted to depict *Roxborough* complete with the colours and design for the camouflaged Second World War version. The box of parts is fairly basic without any photo-etch and so replacing the parts cast on the thin resin wafer and sourcing extra detail is recommended to produce a reasonable result. Peter has also repeated a number of routines present in his build of *Oakley*, with the inclusion of a cut sample of Ikea net curtains seen hung over the side of the ship as part of the rescue attempt. A health warning: parts this small are difficult to see and so Peter uses x2.5 magnification reading glasses from Poundland, UK, without which most of the work would be impossible!

WSW *WESTMINSTER* 1:700 scale

By RAY NOLTON

Ray's model of a WAIR conversion is from the WSW kit. It is entitled 'Into the Wind' and Ray has tried to emulate the sea flattened by the force of the wind.

SCRATCH-BUILT *COTSWOLD*, *BADSWORTH* AND *ROCKWOOD* 1:350 scale

By PHIL REEDER

These three models of the 'Hunt' class destroyers, Type 1 *Cotswold* (L54), Type 2 *Badsworth* (L03) and Type 3 *Rockwood* (L39), clearly show the progression of the design. For the Type 1, Phil used a 200th scale cardboard kit as a reference

and all three were made from plastic card and spares from left over kits. For other references, Phil used the Man O'War book, a World Ship Society book, and plans from an old *Model Maker* magazine. The only after-market parts were stock PE deck railings.

AIRFIX (MIRAGE) *BURNHAM* 1:400 scale

By ROGER THOMAS

The Airfix (ex-Mirage) 1:400 scale model of *Montgomery* formed the basis of the model. This produces a well detailed model straight out of the box, but the kit does not supply railings or fine detail photo-etch, so these will have to be sourced elsewhere. It is not without its problems and, unlike Airfix's skill-rating of '2' emblazoned on the box, the numerous small parts with wide sprue gates, and the flush joints without locating pins are a challenge and require considerable patience and skill; not for the faint-hearted (definitely a skill-rating '4'). It should be noted that the two 1:400 scale 'Town' class 'four-pipers' produced by Airfix are substantially different kits with many differences in details, deckhouses, fittings and armament.

The model represents *Burnham* stripped of its armament, apart from the Hedgehog and most fittings, with a broken keel and a twisted mast, having been driven up onto an improvised hard on the beach at Fort Road, Pembroke Dock, ready for scrapping by Thomas Ward between 1946 and 1947. The ship had been laid up previously with numerous other small warships and escorts awaiting their fate on the mudflats between Lambeeth and Bentlass on Pembroke River, with the paintwork suffering the privations of lack of maintenance and a tidal salt environment. Roger only had black & white photos to determine the colour scheme from and he concluded that it was either the late-war Admiralty Scheme of B30 Dark Olive hull and B55 Medium Grey upperworks, or G45 Light Olive hull and Duck Egg Green upperworks; after some debate, he chose the latter.

Roger will be setting the model in a scenario with a 3D print of the South-West Gun Tower at Pembroke.

DEANS MARINE ***MELBREAK*** 1:96 scale

By RON WILKINSON

Ron produced his model of *Melbreak*, a Batch 3 'Hunt' from the Deans Marine kit of *Tantaside*. It is not made as a static model, but is fully remote controlled, with twin shafts, working navigation lights, searchlights and interior lighting; also 'A' gun mount revolves. He also weathered it to demonstrate the battering the ships got in service. The pom-pom was scratch-built (Ron didn't like the kit one!), the DCT was replaced, the twin 4in mountings were upgraded, as were the ship's boats. Obviously because it is remote controlled, things have to be made a bit more substantial, and access has to be provided to replace the batteries etc.

'Hunt' Type 1, HMS *Liddesdale*,
1942

MS4A B5

'Hunt' Type 2, HMS *Avon Vale*,
1944

G10 G20 G45 B55

'Hunt' Type 3, RHN *Pindos* ex-HMS *Bolebroke*,
1942

Starboard side taken from photos

Port side taken from photos

Copied from Plate 38 – CAFO 679/42

MS1 MS3

‘Hunt’ Type 4, HMS *Brissenden*,
1943

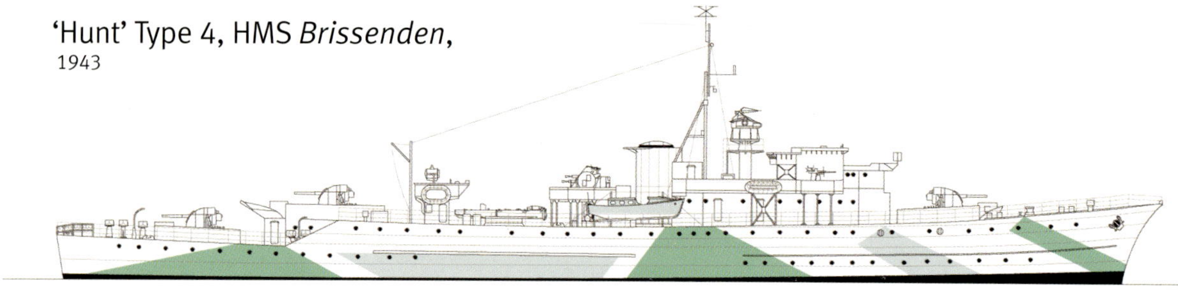

Western Approaches Blue | Western Approaches Green | White

‘Town’ class, HMS *Campbeltown*,
after first stage refit, 1940

Western Approaches Blue | Mountbatten Pink | White

‘Town’ class, HMS *Campbeltown*,
refitted for St Nazaire raid, 1942
Note that while it is known that the ship was painted pink, it is not certain the shade was Mountbatten Pink

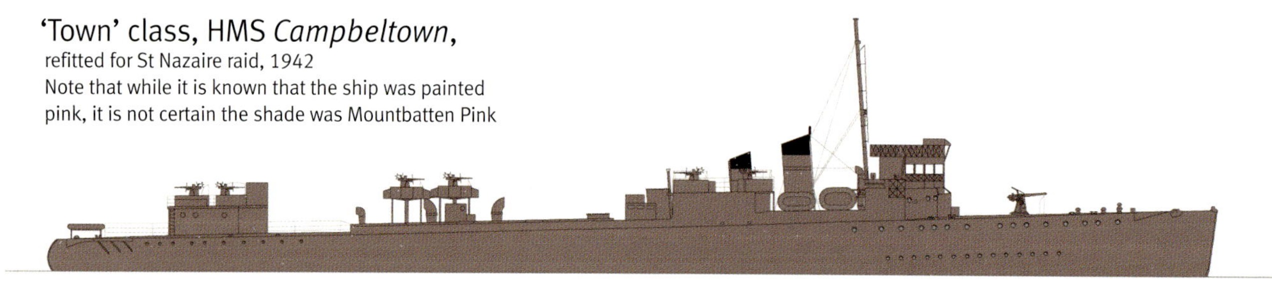

‘Town’ class, HMS *Stanley*,
as Long Range Escort, 1941

Western Approaches Blue | White

'Town' class, HMS *Ludlow*,
as Short Range Escort, 1942
Colours not known

'Town' class, HMS *Ludlow*,
as Short Range Escort, 1943

G10 G45 B55

'Town' class, HMS *Roxborough*,
as Short Range Escort, 1942

Western Approaches Blue Western Approaches Green White

'Town' class, HMS *Roxborough*,
as Short Range Escort, 1943

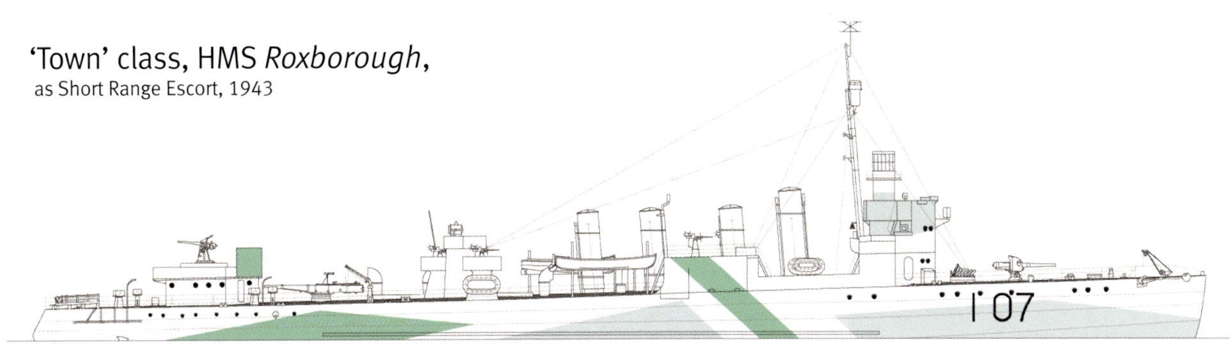

'S' class, HMS *Saladin*,
as escort destroyer, 1943

507C MS4A B5

'V&W' class, HMS *Vansittart*,
as Long Range Escort, 1943

G10 G45 B55

'V&W' class, HMS *Whitshed*,
as Short Range Escort, 1943

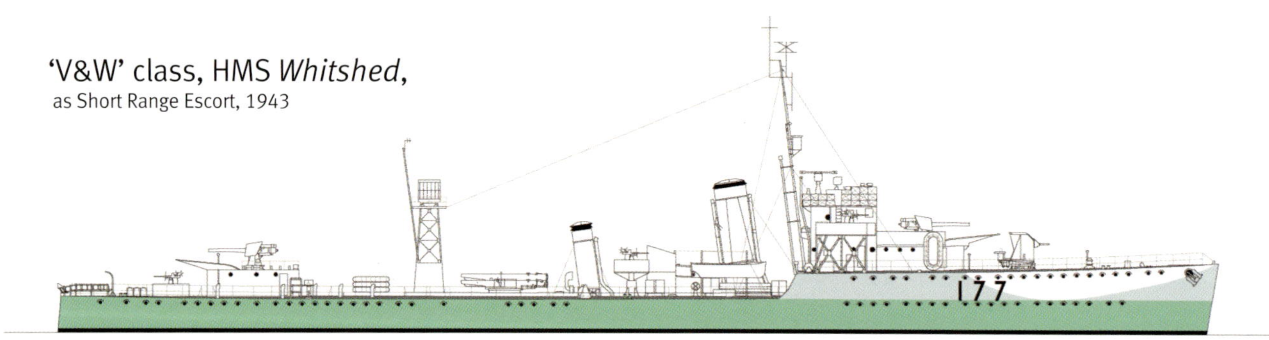

Western Approaches Blue

Western Approaches Green

White

'V&W' class, HMS *Verdun*,
as WAIR conversion, 1942

MS2 MS4 MS4A

CAMOUFLAGE

When first completed many of the 'Hunt' class destroyers were either painted dark grey overall (507A) or had dark grey hulls with light grey upperworks (507C). A number of unofficial schemes appeared in 1940, and in early 1941 Western Approaches schemes began to appear. The scheme worn by *Badsworth* in mid-1940 had its origins in the 'dazzle camouflage' of WWI. *Cotswold* was painted Mountbatten Pink in 1941. Although 1942 brought more general acceptance of the Admiralty standard schemes, some of the destroyers, including *Belvoir* and *Aldenham*, retained one-off schemes.

In general, 'Hunts' operating in the Western Approaches or Arctic wore WA schemes, those operating in the Channel or North Sea wore an Admiralty Light Disruptive scheme, whilst those operating in the Mediterranean had dark hulls with light upperworks. By the time of the Normandy landings, most disruptive schemes had disappeared, and the Admiralty Standard schemes were in general use.

When first commissioned, the majority of 'Town' class destroyers wore a Western Approaches scheme, with a predominately white hull. Usually, patches of the hull were either painted in light blue or green, and in

Above: The Type 3 destroyer *Aldenham* carries a striking pattern, using many small triangular areas.

Left: The Type 1 'Hunt' class destroyer *Cleveland* wears a simple two-colour camouflage scheme. Note the additional Type 271 radar fitted aft. By 1944 she had a tall mainmast carrying a number of radar aerials added just ahead of the quad 2pdr mounting.

Left: Alternatively, here sister ship, *Glaisdale*, has a 'curved' pattern.

Right: The camouflage on the Type 2 destroyer *Badsworth* employs more colours. Note how these colours extend over the bridge, funnel, superstructure and gun platforms.

Right: *Churchill* has a dark fourth funnel and a dark top to her bridge as part of her camouflage pattern. Note how the Type 271 radar lantern above the bridge is much lighter. She has a cowl on her fore funnel, and a HF/DF aerial aft.

Below: *Saladin* wearing an Admiralty Disruptive scheme in 1943.

some cases both. As the war went on, darker patches were introduced, eventually leading to Admiralty Disruptive schemes, the destroyers becoming much darker overall.

At the beginning of the war, the WWI-era vessels were painted medium grey, 507B, with decks of the same colour and corticene. Many received unofficial paint schemes during the early years of the war, later changing to Western Approaches schemes, and later still, to various Admiralty schemes, using primarily a mixture of different greys and blues.

MODIFICATIONS

Records to produce a definitive list of modifications and their dates for smaller vessels either do not exist or, if they do, are difficult to locate. Photographs do allow some configurations to be identified, although in some cases the censor has removed sensitive items. A few details of individual ship configurations, obtained primarily from photographs, are given below. The dates are when the particular configuration was identified, not when the equipment was fitted.

'Hunt' class: None of them received a major upgrade, but radar sets were added to those completed without them, and sensors were frequently upgraded when possible. The first sets fitted were Type 286, which was carried at the foremast head. The array was fixed, requiring the destroyer to turn in order to carry out a search. These were subsequently upgraded to the more powerful Type 290, with a trainable antenna. Late in 1943, some destroyers received the surface warning set Type 271, easily distinguishable by the antenna being sited in a lantern, mounted amidships in lieu of the searchlight, on a structure above the radar office. An IFF antenna was frequently mounted on top of the lantern, as in *Avon Vale*. Type 271 was later replaced by the much smaller Type 268 at the foremast head.

'Hunt' Type 1: Single 20mm Oerlikon guns were fitted in the bridge wings of the Type 1 destroyers when available. *Eridge* had hers fitted lower at the forecastle deck level.

Atherstone received a 2pdr 'bow chaser' in October to November 1941, whilst under repair following weather damage received when escorting a Channel convoy. In 1942, she carried a Type 286 radar at her masthead, but this had been replaced by a Type 291 radar by 1943.

Berkeley carried a Type 291 radar at her masthead in 1943.

Cleveland carried a Type 286 radar at her masthead in 1941 and had her mainmast removed and replaced with a shorter stump mast in November 1942.

Fernie carried a Type 86 VHF radio to communicate with Allied coastal forces and aircraft, antennas to detect German coastal forces transmissions, and a 2pdr 'bow chaser' in January 1943.

Garth had her mainmast removed during a refit in early 1941.

Liddesdale carried a Type 291 radar at her masthead, but no surface search radar in May 1942. She was fitted with a 2pdr 'bow chaser' at that time. By 1942, she had received a Type 286 radar in lieu of the Type 291, and was fitted with antennas to detect German coastal forces transmissions and to communicate with Allied coastal forces and aircraft. She also carried a shielded Lewis gun on the platform aft of the funnel.

Meynell received a twin biaxial 40mm Bofors mounting in lieu of the quadruple pom-pom in 1945.

Whaddon was still waiting to receive her

Below: *Hambledon* was launched at Swan Hunter's shipyard on the same day that *Atherstone* was launched by Cammell Laird, but did not undergo her inclining experiment until after the stability calculation error had been discovered. Here she is seen in August 1945, showing modifications, most noticeable being the Type 271 radar on a tall structure amidships. Note she is painted in the 'peacetime' colour scheme of a dark hull, with the pennant number outlined in white, light upperworks and coloured funnel bands.

20mm guns in February 1941, but she did carry a Mk V** rangefinder director at that time. In 1942, she carried a Type 286 radar at her masthead.

'Hunt' Type 2: *Avon Vale* carried a Type 271 radar in a lantern, with an IFF interrogator on top, on a short tower amidships in 1942. She also had HF/DF on a stump mast aft and a Type 286 radar at her masthead. By 1944 the HF/DF had been removed and the Type 286 radar replaced by a Type 291.

Badsworth carried a Type 291 radar on her mast in 1942.

Blackmore carried Type 286 and Type 271 radars, as well as HF/DF, in 1942.

Blankney carried a Type 286 radar at her masthead in 1941, but did not have a Type 285 radar on her director at that time. By 1942, the Type 285 had been fitted, and a Type 271 radar in a lantern added amidships. The Type 286 radar had been replaced by a Type 291 by 1943.

Bleasdale was converted to act as a headquarters ship for the Normandy landings, with her Type 271 radar in a lantern aft, and a Type 291 radar at her masthead. Her foremast also carried antennas to detect German coastal forces transmissions and to communicate with Allied coastal forces and aircraft.

Cattistock carried a Type 271 radar on a short tower amidships in 1942, but had no radar at her masthead.

Chiddingfold and *Grove* both carried a Type 286 radar at the masthead in 1942.

Croome carried a Type 286 radar at her masthead and a Type 271 radar amidships in 1942, with HF/DF on a stump mast.

Exmoor was similar to *Croome*, but with no HF/DF.

Farndale carried a Type 268 radar at her masthead in February 1947.

Hurworth carried a Type 271 radar in a lantern amidships and Type 286 at her masthead in 1942.

Lamerton carried a Type 286 radar at her foretop, with Type 86 VHF radio for communication with Allied coastal forces and aircraft, above in late 1941. She also carried a 2pdr 'bow chaser'.

Oakley, renamed *Kujawiak* whilst serving with the Free Polish Navy but under RN operational control, carried a Type 286 radar at her masthead in 1941. *Oakley* (ii), originally named *Tickham* but renamed after the first ship was transferred to the Polish Navy, carried a Type 271 radar in 1943.

Puckeridge carried a Type 286PU, rotatable, radar set at her masthead in 1942.

Late in 1943, some of the Type 2 and Type 3 destroyers received twin 20mm mountings instead of the singles. In 1945, the destroyers intended for use in the Far East had their 20mm guns removed and replaced by hand-worked Mk III Bofors 40mm mountings, usually sited before the bridge and on the quarterdeck. The vessels concerned were *Avon Vale, Beaufort, Exmoor, Ledbury,*

Below: The 'bow chaser' gun of *Avon Vale* is protected by a canvas screen. The Type 271 radar is sited amidships on an elevated platform.

Tetcott and *Zetland* (Type 2 destroyers), and *Belvoir, Easton, Haydon, Melbreak* and *Talybont* (Type 3 destroyers).

'Hunt' Type 3: *Aldenham* did not receive her Type 271 radar until sometime after August 1942.

Blean was carrying a Type 286 radar in 1942.

Border, transferred to the Royal Hellenic Navy and renamed *Adrias*, was carrying a Type 291 radar in 1943.

Easton was carrying a Type 272 radar (an improved and smaller Type 271) and a Type 291 at her masthead in 1943. She also had an additional 20mm gun on her quarterdeck at that time. She received a Type 650 jamming antenna next to the lantern in 1944. When modified for service in the Pacific (May to August 1945), not only did she have her armament changed from 20mm to 40mm, but also received radar Type 268 at her masthead, replacing the Type 272.

Eggesford was carrying both Type 271 and Type 286 radars in 1943.

Haydon was carrying a Type 286 radar in 1943 but this was later replaced by a Type 291.

Haldon was transferred to the Free French Navy, being renamed *La Combattante*, and carried a Type 291 radar in 1944. She was lost in 1945.

Melbreak was carrying a Type 286 radar in 1942.

'Hunt' Type 4: Both *Brissenden* and *Brecon* carried a Type 291 radar. *Brissenden* received twin power-operated 20mm Oerlikons in the bridge wings when refitted at Malta in April/June 1946.

'Town' class: Further modifications were carried out to most vessels over time; the beam 4in guns were removed and replaced with 20mm Oerlikon guns, the forward torpedo tubes were replaced by a centreline triple mounting and radar was added (Type 286 at the masthead and Type 271 on the bridge top). The majority also received a Hedgehog mortar and HF/DF equipment, the antennas being mounted on a tall mast aft.

Here are a few details of individual ships, after further modifications:

Annapolis (ex-*Mackenzie*) carried a SW1C radar at her masthead, in lieu of the

Above: This 1947 view of *Easton* (Type 3) shows the 40mm Mk III gun in front of the bridge. Note she is not carrying the Type 272 radar fitted previously.

Below: *Brissenden* leaving Malta in 1946.

Above: This view of *Annapolis* shows the remaining three funnels. Type 271 radar is fitted on the bridge with the SW1C radar at her masthead.

Below: *Campbeltown* undergoing modification for the raid on the port of St Nazaire. Note the cut-down funnels with raked tops, and the 20mm Oerlikon guns fitted alongside the funnels and on the platform aft.

Type 286, in 1941. Her Hedgehog was fitted on the starboard side, and her aft funnel had been removed after the boiler had burnt out.

Broadwater (ex-*Mason*) carried a Hedgehog mortar forward and 20mm guns abreast the funnels in early 1942 but retained 0.5in machine guns on the bandstand aft. She was later converted to an Air Target ship, when most of the previous modifications were removed and two heavy davits fitted.

Burnham (ex-*Aulick*) carried a third 20mm gun instead of her searchlight in the third quarter of 1942, together with both Type 271 and 286 radars, and centreline torpedo tubes.

Campbeltown (ex-*Buchanan*) receive a

major refit for the attack on the dock gates at St Nazaire in 1942, the aft two funnels being removed and the forward two reduced in height with raked tops to resemble the German *Möwe* class torpedo boats. A 12pdr gun was mounted on the forecastle.

Leeds (ex-*Conner*) carried a 12pdr forward in 1942, the 2pdr guns previously fitted having been used to replace the beam 3in mountings.

Lincoln (ex-*Yarnell*) received a Type 291 radar at her masthead and Type 271 on her bridge roof. She also carried Hedgehog forward, centreline torpedo tubes and 20mm guns abeam the funnels. In 1943, she landed her port boat.

Mansfield (ex-*Evans*) carried Type 286 and 271 radars, with Hedgehog forward, in 1942.

Montgomery (ex-*Wickes*) received an additional pair of 20mm guns on a bandstand, near the searchlight.

Newark (ex-*Ringgold*) received Type 271 and 291 radars during a refit in late 1942.

Niagara (ex-*Thatcher*) retained her beam 4in guns but had a centreline torpedo tube mounted, and the height of her after funnels reduced. Type 271 radar was not added until January 1943.

Ramsey (ex-*Meade*) received a Type 271 radar in a lantern on the bridge, but otherwise was similar to *Newport* after her initial modifications, although she did not have any 20mm Oerlikon guns.

Richmond (ex-*Fairfax*) received Hedgehog, Type 271 radar, centreline torpedo tubes and HF/DF on a pole mast aft. The beam 4in guns were replaced with 20mm mountings, which were also added on a bandstand near the searchlight.

Ripley (ex-*Shubrick*) and *Roxborough* (ex-*Foote*), in addition to the Type 271 radar, received a Hedgehog mortar forward of the bridge, four depth charge throwers and 20mm Oerlikon guns, three and four, respectively. *Ripley* received a cap to her fore funnel, had her searchlight moved to between funnels 2 and 3 and replaced by 20mm guns. She had an HF/DF aerial on a pole mast aft in late 1943.

St Albans (ex-*Thomas*) had Type 271 and 291 radars in 1942. She retained her beam 4in guns and her US 3in gun forward of the bridge, aft of the forward mounting, but no torpedo tubes. She later had her beam guns replaced by 20mm mountings, and 20mm guns were added, replacing the searchlight and aft of the fourth funnel. She also carried a triple torpedo tube mounting.

St Croix (ex-*McCook*) carried a triple torpedo tube mounting, whilst retaining her beam 4in guns, in 1942. She was fitted with a radar Type SW1C at the time.

St Francis (ex-*Bancroft*) received a Type 271 radar, had her bridge rebuilt and her torpedo tubes removed. The beam 4in guns were replaced with 20mm mountings, and her third boiler and funnel were removed.

Salisbury (ex-*Claxton*) received the Type 271 radar, HF/DF equipment, triple torpedo tubes and 20mm guns but, in July 1942, she was without Hedgehog.

Those that operated as East Coast convoy escorts frequently had all their original armament removed, and received just a single depth charge rail and two throwers. *Lewes* (ex-*Conway*) and *Ludlow* (ex-*Stockton*) both received three 3in/50cal mountings, one on the quarterdeck and two in lieu of the beam 4in mountings, two 2pdr mountings side-by-side, forward of the bridge, and two 20mm guns on platforms forward of the aft superstructure. The searchlight was relocated to the aft superstructure and the foremast was fitted with Type 291 and Type 286 AW radars, respectively.

'V&W' class: Those SRE conversions that were used primarily as escorts for East Coast convoys, including *Mackay*, *Walpole*, *Whitshed*, *Windsor* and *Wivern*, had their forward mounting replaced by a twin 6pdr Mk 1 mounting.

Venomous underwent conversion between January and March 1942, when she received a Type 271 radar.

Witherington received Type 271 radar between March and August 1942.

Wild Swan had her aft torpedo tubes replaced by a 12pdr AA gun during a refit in June 1940. By 1942/3, she carried an HF/DF mast aft, and her 2pdr guns had been replaced by 20mm guns.

Veteran was under refit in February 1941 and received MF/DF Outfit FM7 as an aid to navigation. In January 1942, she received another refit and conversion for use as a Short Range Escort.

In 1942/3, *Vivacious* carried both Type 271 and 291 radars, two main gun mountings, 'A' having been replaced by Hedgehog, a 12pdr AA mounting and four 20mm guns.

Vortigern underwent conversion between September and November 1940. In 1941/2 she carried a Type 276 radar at her masthead, 'Y' gun had been replaced by depth charges and her aft torpedo tubes by a 12pdr AA gun. She also had two single 2pdr guns just aft of the funnels and 20mm guns on the bridge wings.

In 1942, *Wivern* carried Type 291 radar at her masthead, replacing Type 276 and Type 271 amidships on a lattice mast. She also carried an HF/DF mast aft.

In 1943, *Witch* had received a Hedgehog mortar and Type 291 radar. She retained two 2pdr guns between the funnels but had 20mm guns on the bridge wings.

By 1942, *Viceroy*, a WAIR conversion, was carrying a Type 271 radar on a short lattice mast amidships, with 2pdr guns on a platform just in front. *Vanity* also carried Type 271 on a similar mast, but did not have the 2pdr guns, just four 20mm guns. At this time, *Vega* had a HF/DF mast aft, and carried Type 286P radar on her mast.

Wolfhound carried Type 271 radar on a short lattice mast in 1941, as did *Winchester* in 1942, although she had still not received

Below: *Veteran*, pictured in February 1942, retains 'B' and 'X mountings and one set of triple torpedo tubes. A 12pdr AA gun is sited aft of the searchlight tower, two single 2pdr mountings are sited between the funnels, and Type 271 radar is fitted to the bridge roof.

Above, left: The Type 272 radar lantern is clear in this photograph of *Wallace*, as is the quadruple 2pdr pom-pom on the platform at the stern. At this time, she is still carrying quad 0.5in machine gun mounts.

Above, right: *Shikari* carried a Type 272 radar on a tall lattice mast at the end of the war.

a Type 285 fire control radar. *Woolston* was similar but did have a Type 285 radar, and two additional 2pdr mountings immediately forward of the short lattice mast.

In 1944, *Valorous* carried a Type 291 radar at the masthead and a HF/DF mast aft. Her light AA armament comprised four 20mm guns.

'R' class: By the time of the landings in Normandy, *Skate* had had received a Type 271 radar on a lattice mast aft. AA armament was a 12pdr amidships, with two 20mm guns between the second and third funnel, and two on the bridge wings. Type 291 radar was fitted at the masthead.

'S' class: Type 286 radar was added in 1941, but the additional weight of the lower frequency Type 271, precluded it from being fitted. *Shikari* did receive a lower frequency Type 272 radar in 1944, but only after her 12pdr gun was removed and her ASW equipment reduced. The ASW equipment on the others was also reduced, four depth charge throwers being removed, and Mk IV throwers being fitted in place of the original Mk II. Four single 20mm Oerlikon guns replaced the two 0.5in mountings to enhance their AA defence.

'Shakespeare' class flotilla leaders: By late 1942, *Wallace*'s close-in anti-aircraft armament had been enhanced by the addition of two Oerlikon 20mm guns, while Type 272 surface search radar was mounted on a short lattice tower aft, Type 291 air warning radar was mounted at the top of the foremast, and Type 285 gunnery control radar was fitted to the anti-aircraft director. The quadruple 0.5in mounts were later (by mid-1944) replaced by two single 2pdr pom-poms, while two more single Oerlikon 20mm guns were added.

Below: In this profile of *Wallace*, the Type 271 radar, on a lattice tower, stands out very clearly.

'Hunt' Type 1, HMS *Tynedale*,
as completed, 1940

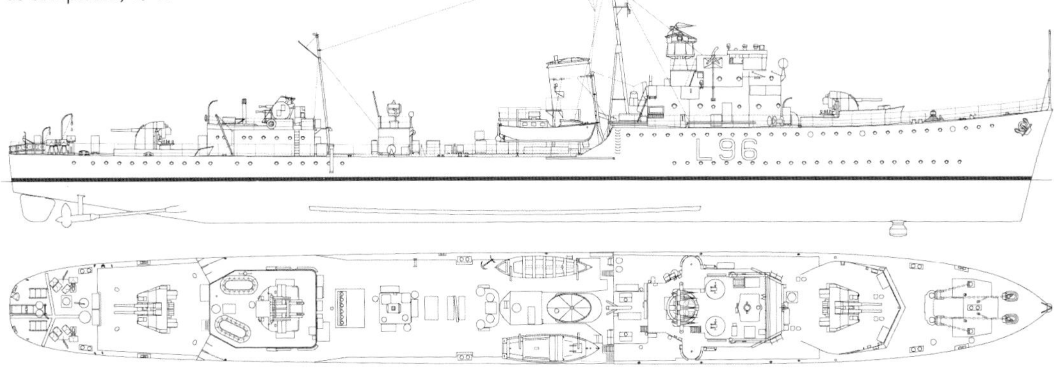

'Hunt' Type 2, HMS *Grove*,
1942

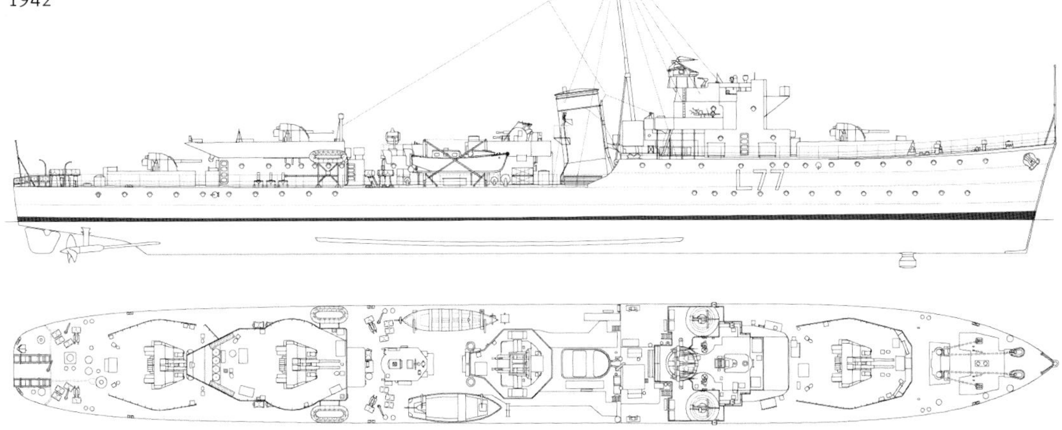

'Hunt' Type 3, HMS *Belvoir*,
as completed, 1942

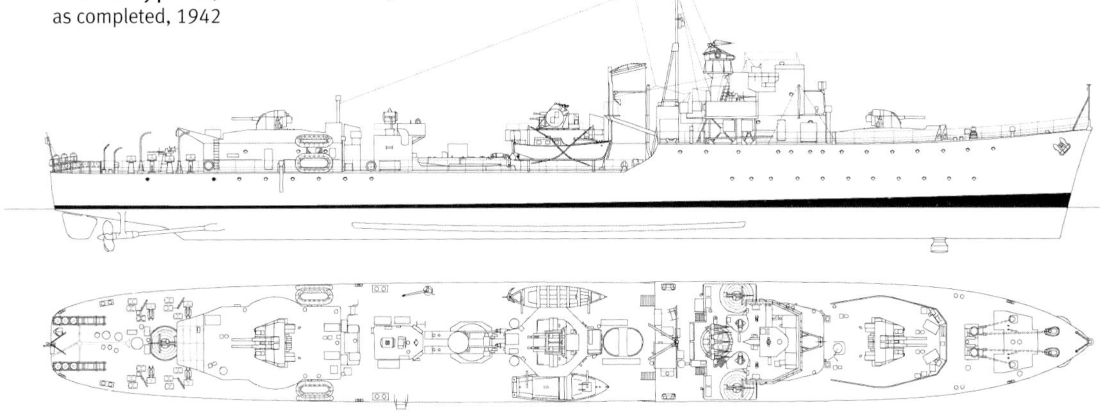

'Hunt' Type 4, HMS *Brissenden*,
as completed, 1943

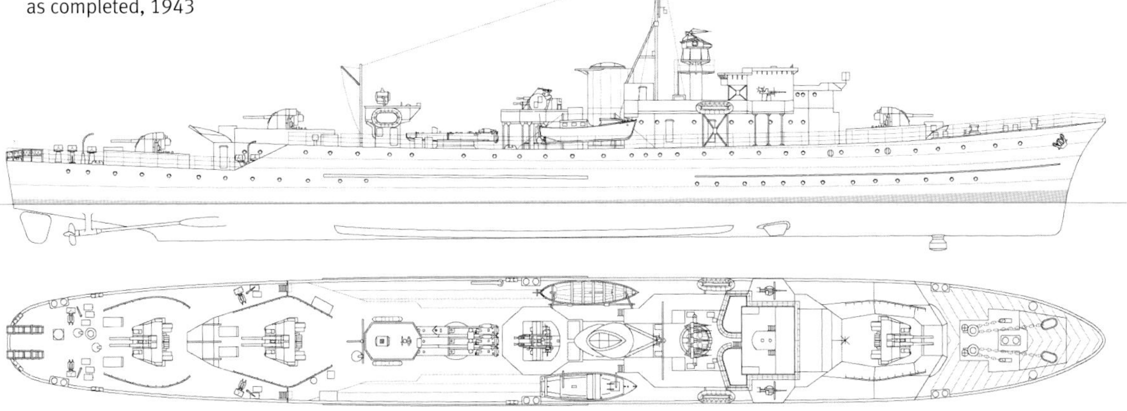

Caldwell class, USS *Stockton* (DD73)

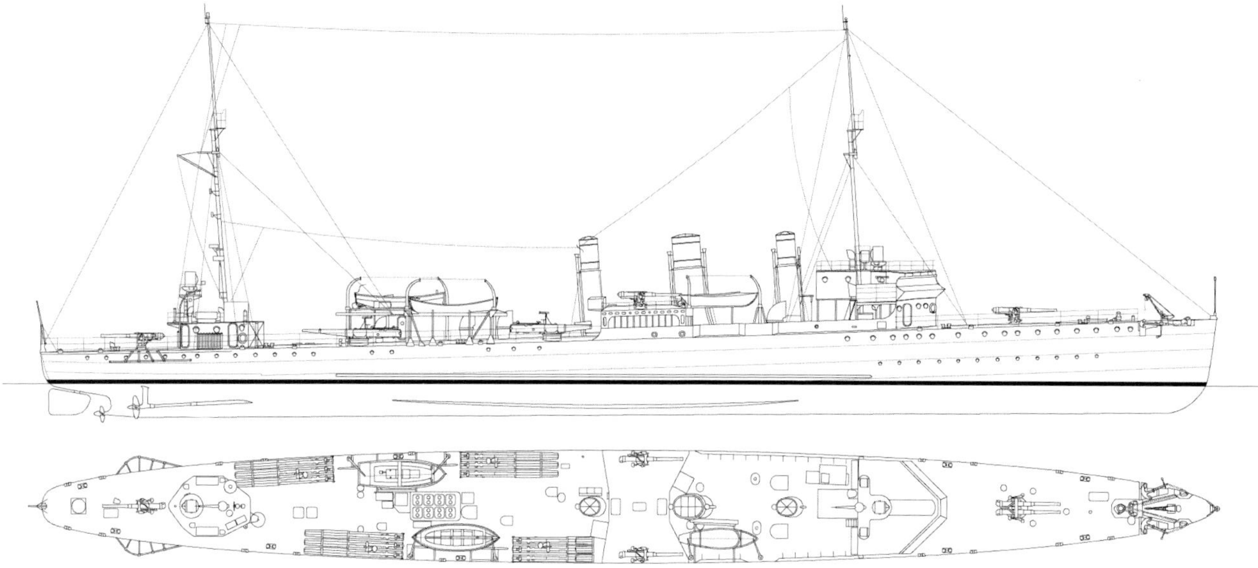

Wickes class, USS *Dyer* (DD84)

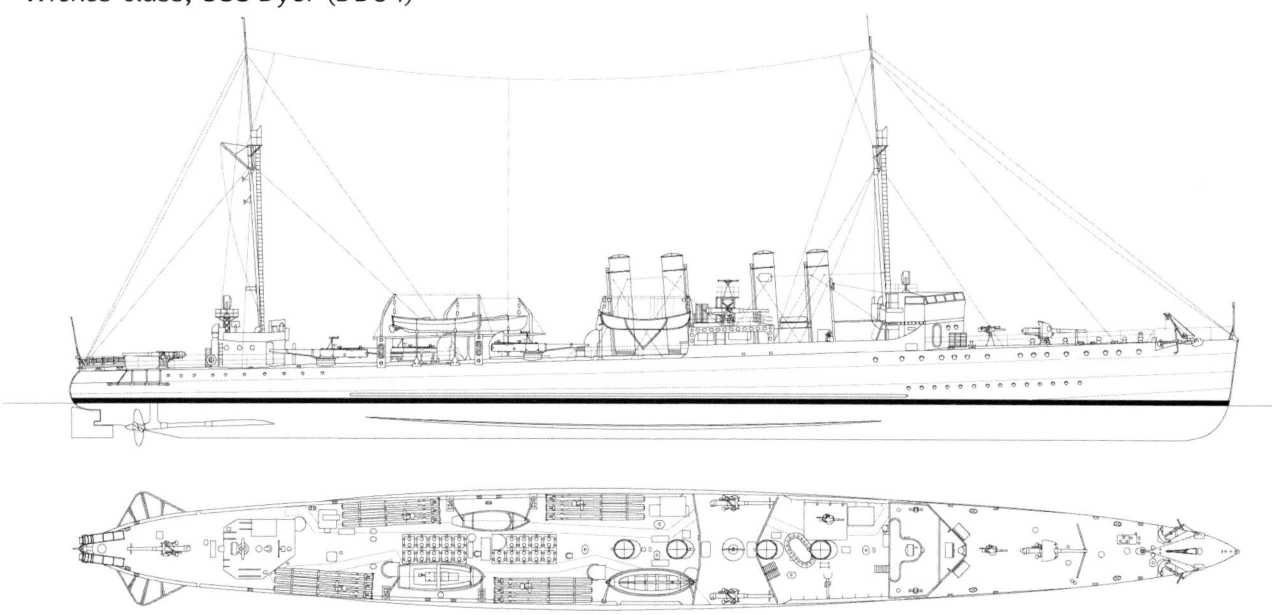

Wickes class, USS *Thomas* (DD182)

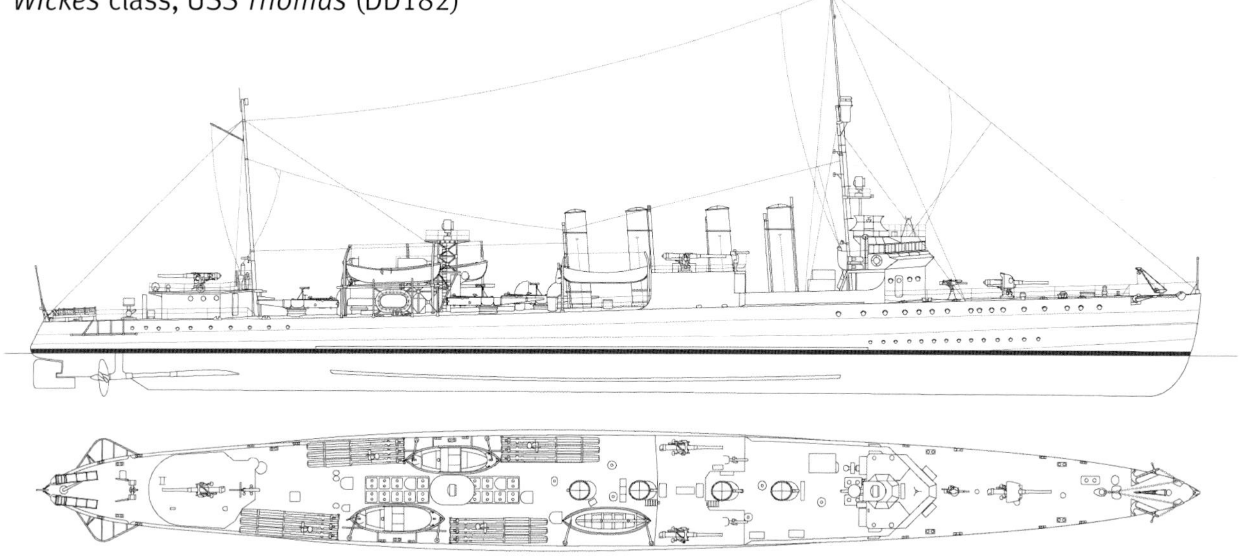

'Town' class, HMS *Roxl*
as Short Range Escort, 1942

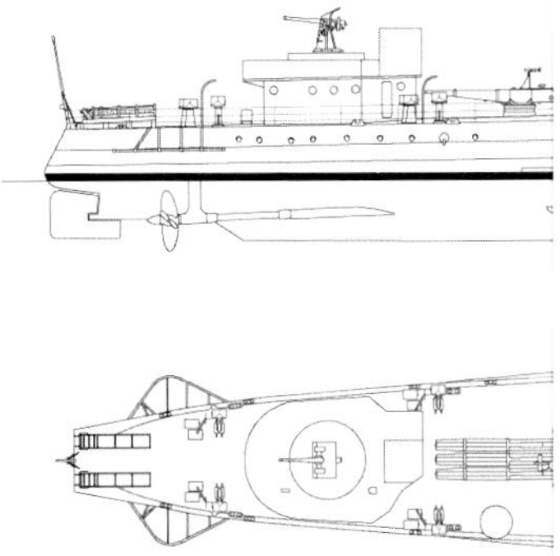

'S' class, HMS *Trojan*,
as completed, 1918

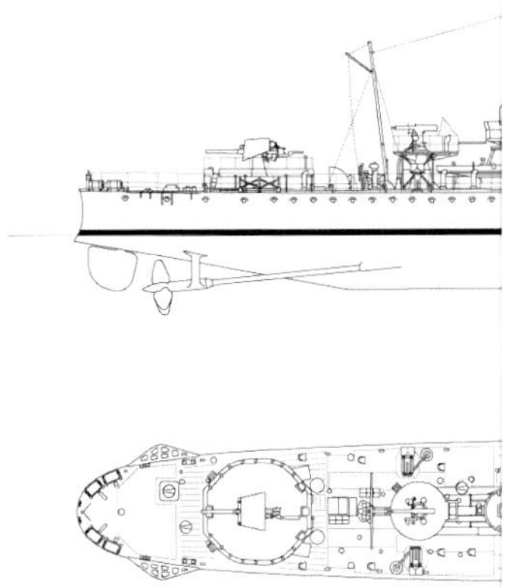

'S' class, HMS *Saladin*
as escort destroyer, 1943

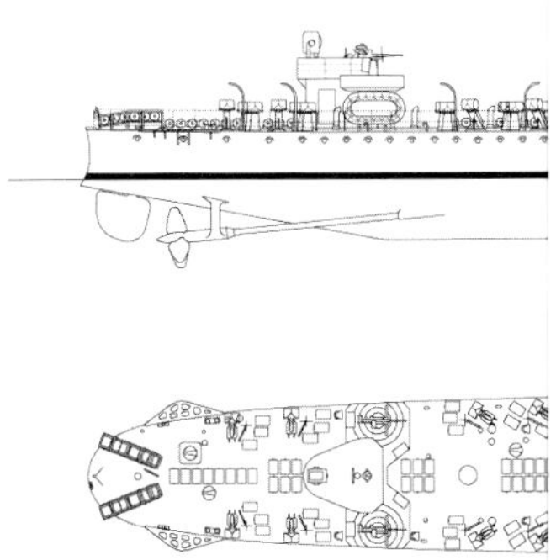

Clemson class, USS *Smith-Thompson* (DD212)

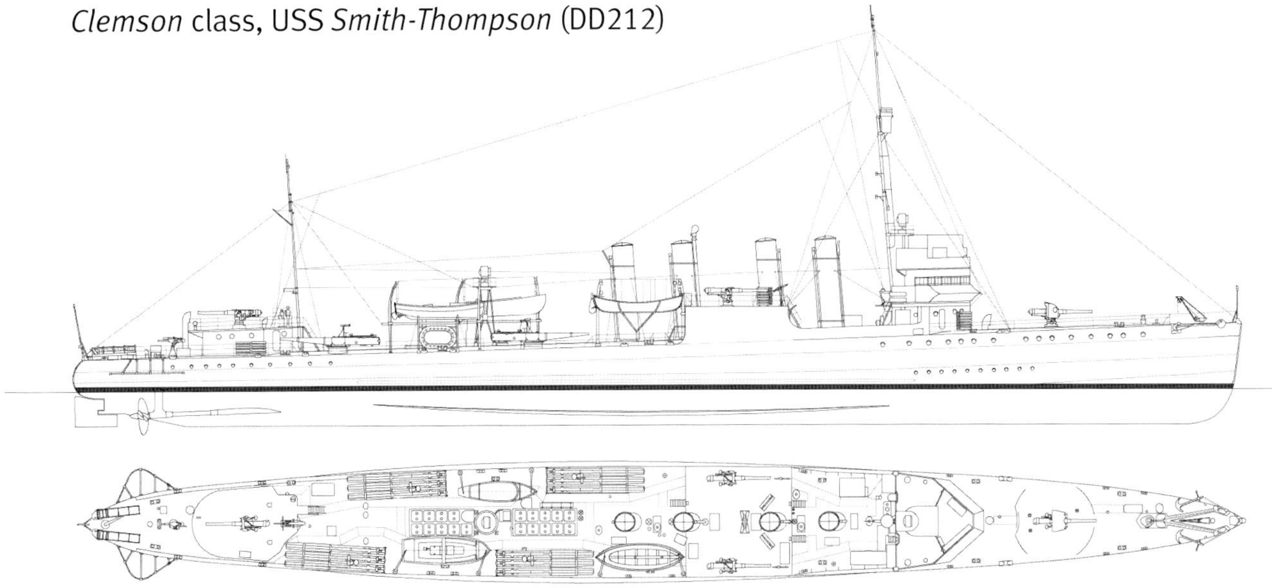

'Town' class, HMS *Campbeltown*,
after first stage refit, 1940

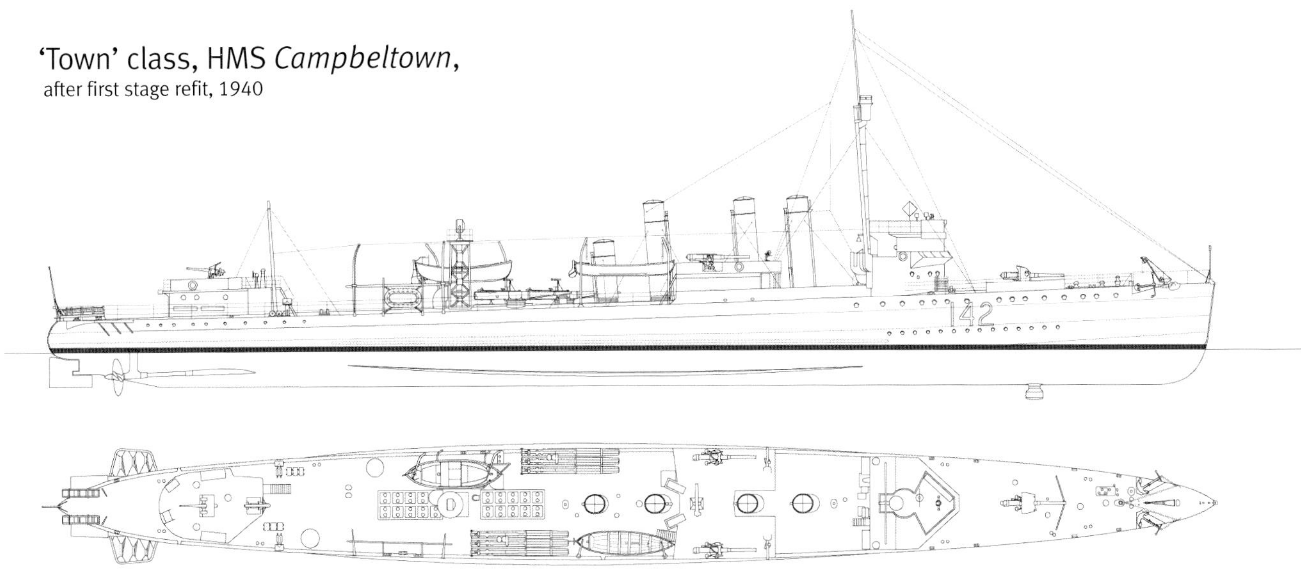

'Town' class, HMS *Campbeltown*,
refitted for St Nazaire raid, 1942

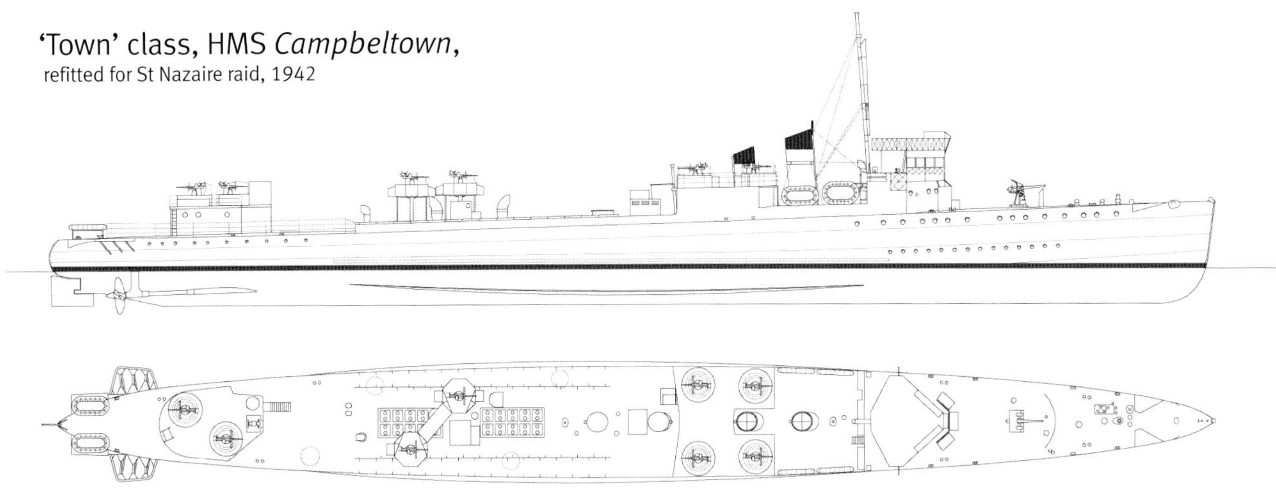

(All drawings by George Richardson)

'Town' class, HMS *St*
as Long Range Escort, 1941

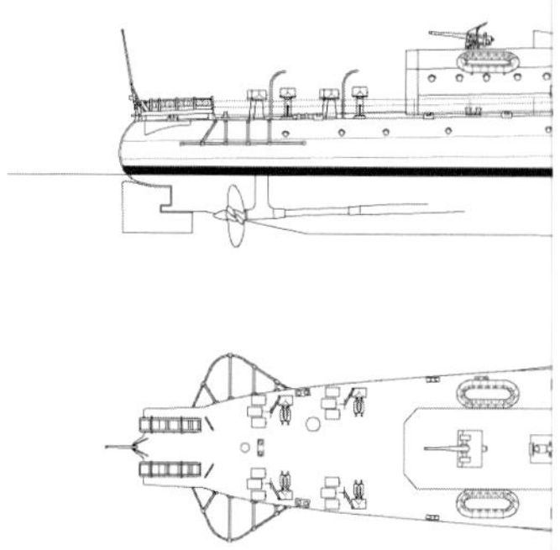

'Town' class, HMS *Lu*
as Short Range Escort, 1942

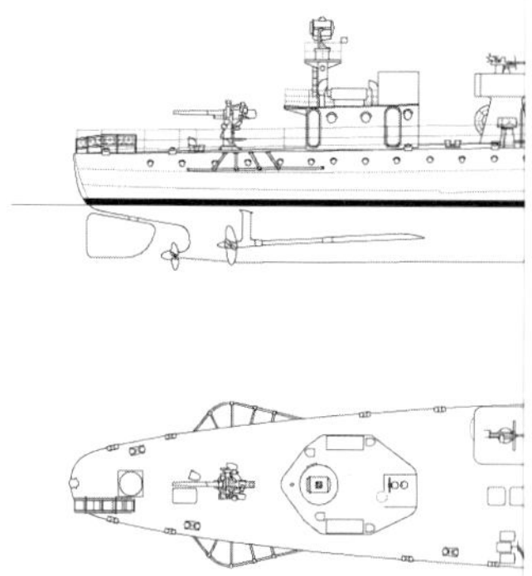

'Town' class, HMS *Lu*
as Short Range Escort, 1943

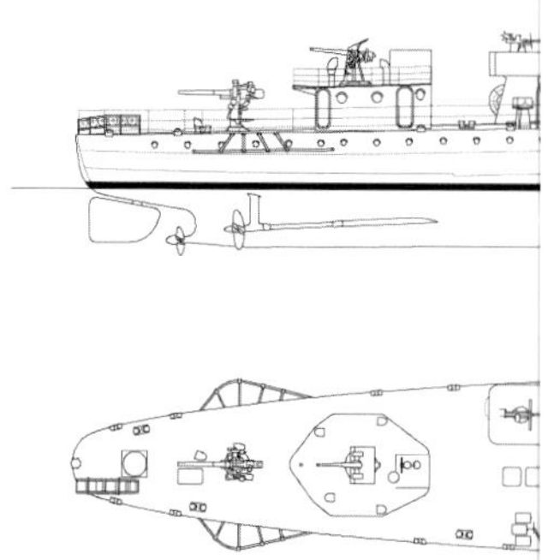

'V&W' class, HMS *Whitehall*,
as completed, 1924

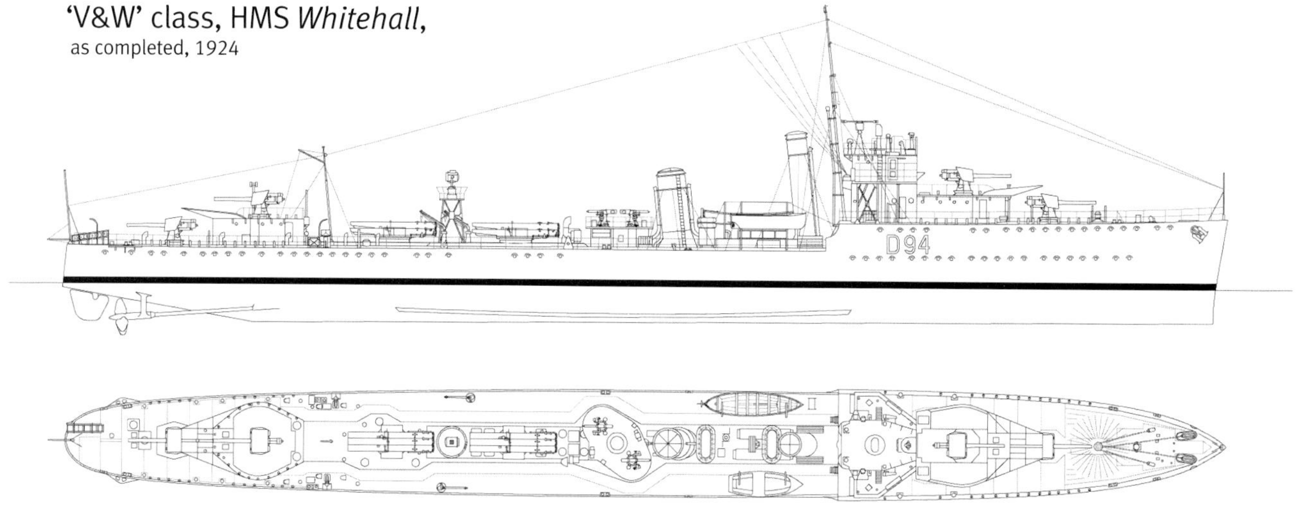

'V&W' class, HMS *Wild Swan*,
as completed, 1919

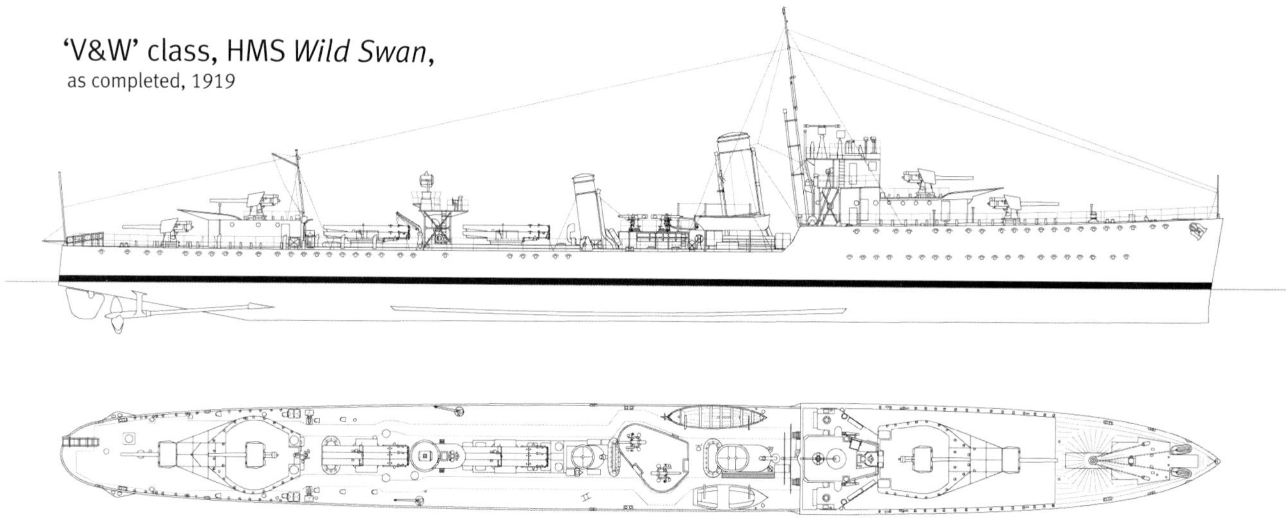

'V&W' class, HMS *Wolfhound*,
as completed, 1918

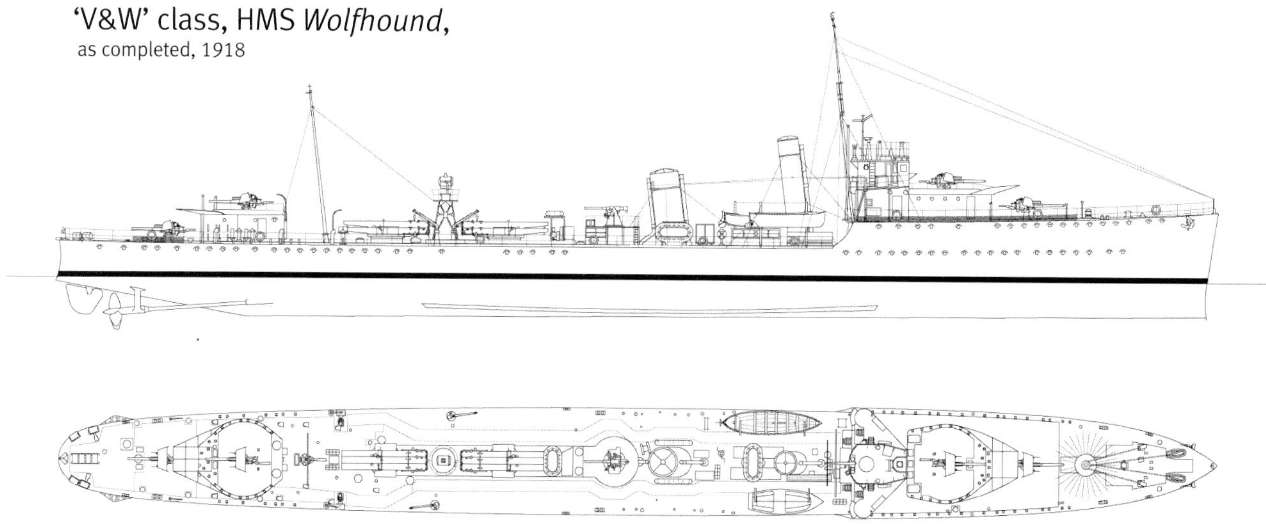

'V&W' class, HMS *Vansittart*,
as Long Range Escort, 1943

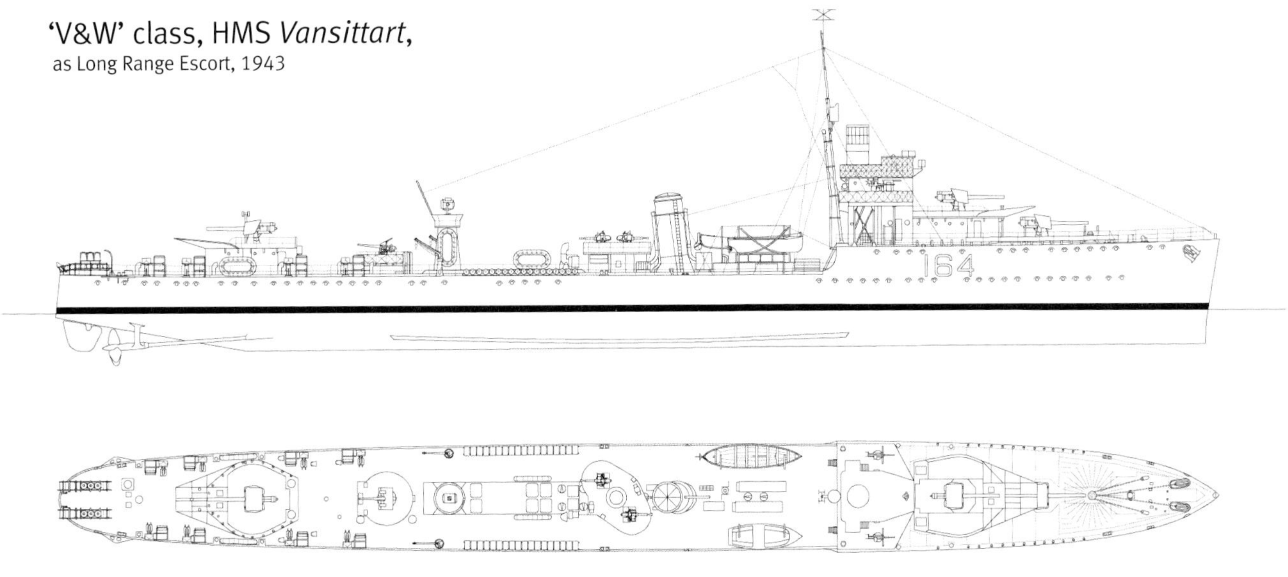

'V&W' class, HMS *Whitshed*,
as Short Range Escort, 1943

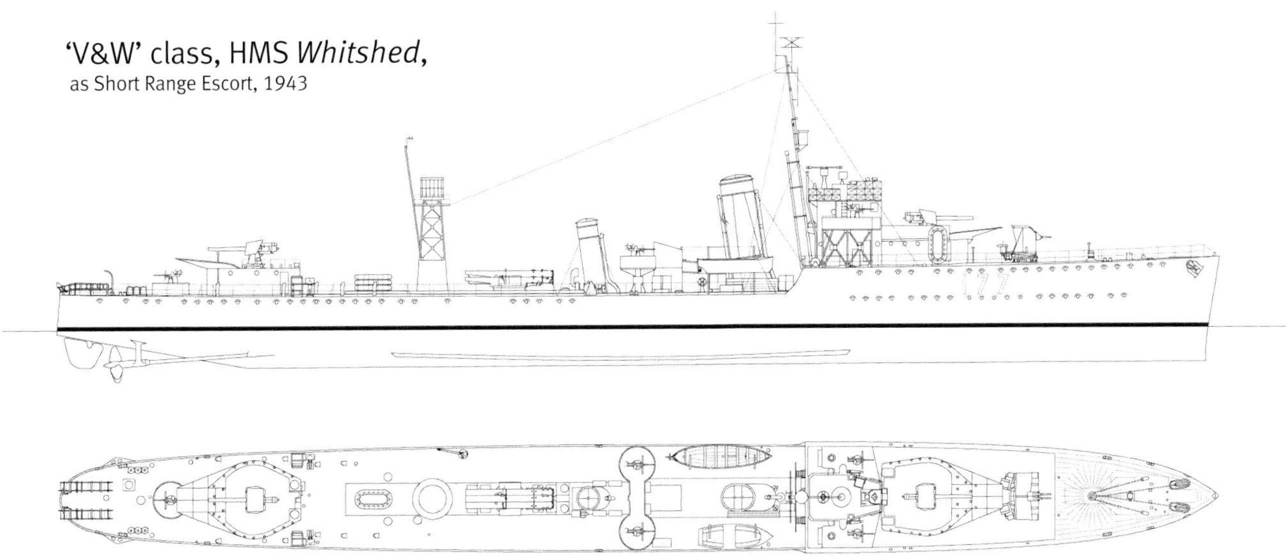

'V&W' class, HMS *Winchester*,
as WAIR conversion, 1940

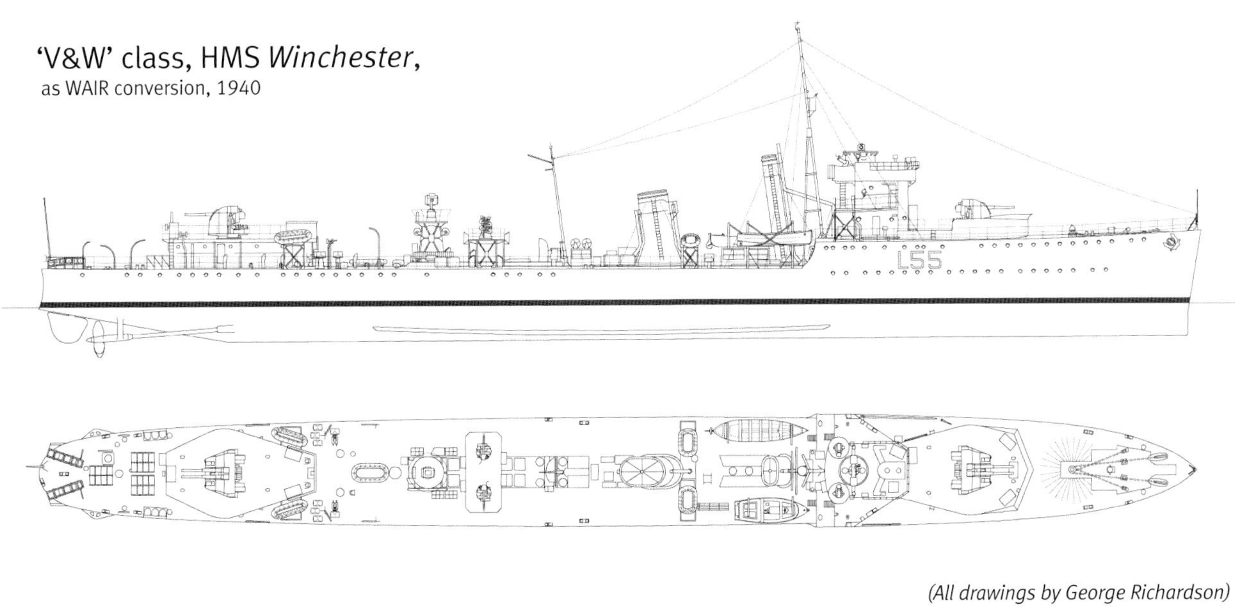

(All drawings by George Richardson)

Selected References

BIBLIOGRAPHY

Anatomy of the Ship: The Destroyer Campbeltown, by Al Ross (Conway Maritime Press, 1990)

British and Commonwealth Warship Camouflage of WWII, (Destroyers, Frigates, Escorts), by Malcolm Wright (Seaforth Publishing, 2014)

British and Empire Warships of the Second World War, by H T Lenton (Greenhill Books, 1998)

British Destroyers & Frigates, by Norman Friedman (Seaforth Publishing, 2006)

British Destroyers 1892–1953, by Edgar J March (Seeley Service,1966)

British Naval Weapons. The John Lambert Collection, Volume I: Destroyer Weapons, edited and introduced by Norman Friedman (Seaforth Publishing, 2019)

British Naval Weapons. The John Lambert Collection, Volume II: Escort and Minesweeper Weapons, edited and introduced by Norman Friedman (Seaforth Publishing, 2019)

Conway's All The World's Fighting Ships 1906-1921, edited by Robert Gardiner (Conway Maritime Press, 1985)

Conway's All The World's Fighting Ships 1922-1946, edited by Robert Gardiner (Conway Maritime Press, 1980)

Destroyers for Great Britain, by Arnold Hague (Greenhill Books, 1990)

Flush Decks and Four Pipes, by John D Alden (United States Naval Institute, 1965)

Grand Fleet Destroyers, by John English (World Ship Society, 2019)

Hunt-class Destroyers in Polish Navy Service, by Mariusz Borowiak (Kagero Publishing)

Man O'War 2: 'V' and 'W' class Destroyers, by Alan Raven & John Roberts (Arms & Armour Press,1979)

Man O'War 4: The 'Hunt' class Escort Destroyers, by Alan Raven & John Roberts (Arms & Armour Press, 1980)

The British Hunt-class Escort Destroyer HMS Badsworth, by Waldemar Góralski (Kagero Publishing)

The Hunts, by John English (World Ship Society, 1987)

Town class Destroyers, by John Henshaw (Crowood Press, 2018)

U.S. Destroyers, by Norman Friedman (Naval Institute Press, 2004)

V & W Destroyers: A Developmental History, by John Henshaw (Seaforth Publishing, 2020)

V and W class Destroyers 1917-1945, by Antony Preston (Macdonald & Co, 1971)

Warship Perspectives: Flush Deck Destroyers in World War Two, by Glenn R Arnold (WR Press Inc, 2001)

MODELLING WEBSITES

www.starling-models.co.uk – UK manufacturer of resin kits and etched brass detail sets, and supplier of a wide range of plastic and resin kits and accessories from international manufacturers.

https://www.atlanticmodels.net – UK manufacturer of resin kits and etched brass detail sets, including many kits previously produced by White Ensign Models (UK).

https://blackcatmodels.eu – French manufacturer of resin kits and 3D printed accessories

www.ironshipwrights.com – US manufacturer of resin kits

www.tomsmodelworks.com – US manufacturer of etched brass accessories

www.whiteensignmodels.com – US manufacturer of etched brass accessories

www.ajmmodels.pl – Polish manufacturer of resin kits and accessories

www.neptunia-hobbies.com – UK manufacturer of card models

www.deansmarine.co.uk – UK manufacturer of radio control kits and accessories

www.nikomodel.pl/index.php/en – Polish manufacturer of resin kits and accessories

ACKNOWLEDGEMENTS

Thanks to all those modellers who provided photographs of their models for inclusion in the Showcase section, with particular thanks to Dave Eyles (solent-modelconstruction.co.uk) for constructing three of the review kits for inclusion, also. Many thanks to Graeme Price for providing photographs of those kits no longer in production.

Right: Two photographs of the twin 6pdr Mk 1 mounting aboard *Mackay*. These rapid-fire guns were fitted in lieu of 'A' mounting to provide more effective engagement of *schnellboote*, and other small craft, which frequently operated against East Coast convoys.